REBEKAH'S DIARY

Rebekah Pearl

A NO GREATER JOY MINISTRIES BOOK

REBEKAH'S DIARY

All Scripture quotations are taken from the King James Holy Bible.

Published by No Greater Joy Ministries
1000 Pearl Road
Pleasantville, TN 37033

www.NoGreaterJoy.org

ISBN-13: 978-1-892112-02-6

First Printing: October 1997
Second Printing: February 2000
Third Printing: August 2008

Cover design: Clint Cearly

Printed in the United States of America

AUTHOR'S NOTE

The role I play in this diary is but a very small part of the whole picture in which many, many people are involved. There are grandparents that pray and support, parents that handle every aspect of the ministry in the U.S. and bear my burdens, siblings that help in any way they can, relatives and Church members that take a personal interest in dozens of creative ways, friends that correspond and pray, and scores of children that write to say they are following behind me. There are so many of you out there that I have never even met who have an active part in God's work among the Kumboi people. Because of you, an island in the South Pacific is being reached with the gospel of Jesus Christ. As you read this diary, may you be inspired to pray with a greater fervency for laborers on the field; may you be inspired to go.

Rebekah Pearl

Rebekah Pearl

Introduction

Rebekah is the oldest child of Michael and Debi Pearl. Her home-school days were continually interrupted with the busy atmosphere of a home dedicated to serving God and others. She grew up seeing the power of God at work transforming the lives of broken sinners.

At seventeen, having never been away from the protective environment of a loving home, she boarded a plane with several other young people and went to South America where she witnessed the power of God transforming the lives of primitive tribal people. She would never be the same. The following year, selling the family cow to raise the last of the money, the Pearls sent their eighteen-year-old daughter to Papua New Guinea. Eight weeks later she came home with a heaven born vision. She would go to linguistic school to learn to translate Scripture into the language of a primitive tribe.

After three years of preparation and much prayer, she boarded a plane for the Madang region of Papua New Guinea. She did not go out under a mission board. She was sent out by her local church. Her eighteen-year-old brother, Gabriel, went along as her "protector." During their four week trip, God led them to the Kumboi people. They returned to the U.S. so she could get an extended visa and make preparation for residency in P.N.G.

She soon returned to the Kumboi. This time, with her seventeen-year-old brother Nathan went along as her assistant. After three months, he came home, leaving her alone on the top of a mountain among tribal people where no white person had ever been. She had no support team, and for the first few months, she had no communication with the outside world. There are no roads to the village. The only way in or out is a six hour hike from a primitive bush air strip.

This is her diary, as she wrote it, from the heights and depths of service to her God.

Papua New Guinea, July

July 9, 1995
[Rebekah, in the city of Port Moresby, just arrived in Papua New Guinea]
"Keep me as the apple of the eye, hide me under the shadow of thy wings."
Psalm 17:8

It has been a full day. Mom just called. It is 7:00 in the morning there, and folks are praying for us. I am still trying to catch up on my sleep.

All the natives think Gabriel is older than I. He leaves them in awe—his height, I guess. The girls come up to stroke my hair and touch my hands. I had to sign my name in the front of nearly 50 Bibles. They are all musical. The guys play the guitar, and they all sing harmonies. It is beautiful. One of them thanked God he was born a New Guinean—born where he could hear the gospel and read his Bible. They are thankful, joyful people.

It is beginning to dawn on me just how dangerous a thing I am attempting to do. I see fear for me in the faces of the P.N. Guineans. Steve Lindsey [missionary there in Moresby] looked at me today and said, "You're crazy. You are stark raving mad. You know they will steal from you, beat you, rape you, and make you wish you were dead, and then they will kill you. It is an absolute impossibility! The only thing that makes me believe that you will survive is knowing that it sounds just like something God would do. And if God is with you, who can be against you?" It gives me chills to remember his face when he said that. God help me. It is now 11:30 P.M. Goodnight.

July 10, 1995
"As for me, I will behold thy face in righteousness: I shall be satisfied, when I awake, with thy likeness." Psalm 17:15

This afternoon, a New Guinean girl named Cathy came to talk to me. She is 25 years old, and got saved 7 years ago. For the last year, she has felt God wanted her to be a missionary to her own country, and she has been praying for a family or another girl to go with her. When she heard me talk about going to the Madang region, she said she thought, "God, could it be that you want me to go with this white girl and serve with her?" She lay awake all night praying, and decided to talk to me. She wants to quit her job at the Post Office and go with me anywhere God leads. She speaks fluent Pidgin, English, and her own tribal language. She knows the Papua

New Guinean culture well. The church in Moresby will support her finan-
cially. We have decided to pray for each other and correspond for a year. It
looks to be God's perfect answer to prayer. I never dreamed I would have a
Papua New Guinean for a partner. The Lindseys are thrilled. They say that
Cathy has a solid testimony and walks righteously with God. All my weaknesses would be her strong points and all her weaknesses are my strong
points. Tomorrow morning we will leave for Madang.

July 11, 1995
     I am sitting in the Port Moresby airport waiting for flight PX 210.
The plane is late, as usual. Across from me is a native family. The little girl
found some bright pink nail polish somewhere, and is now patiently paint-
ing the toes and fingernails of everyone in her family. Both her brothers
and her dad have bright pink nails. How funny!
     I hope the Williamses will be there to pick us up.

July 12, 1995
     When we arrived at the Madang hangar, there was no one there to
meet us. [They came after a while.]

July 13, 1995
*"For thou wilt light my candle: the LORD my God will enlighten my dark-
ness. For by thee I have run through a troop; and by my God have I leaped
over a wall." Psalm 18:28-29*
     At two P.M., Pastor Allen Gami Akij from the Simbai area came to talk
to me. He speaks the Kumboi language and is an important leader among
his people. Allen came out of the bush years ago and learned Pidgin. Then
he got saved and took the gospel message back to his own people in the
mountains. From what I understand, a few have gotten saved and a small
church started. But they have no Bible, and almost none of them can read
or write. Very few have even heard the gospel. When I told Pastor Allen
that I wanted to translate a Bible in tok ples (tribal language), he got excited and asked Bro. Jerry in Pidgin, "Does this mean we will have a Bible in
our language now?" So Monday we are flying out to the Kenanj airstrip and
will hike from village to village and do a language survey. God is leading.

July 17, 1995
*"He maketh my feet like hinds feet and setteth me upon my high places."
Psalm 18:33*
     I'm here! We took a small plane, 5 seater, single prop, turbo, for
35 minutes inland. We flew past the highest mountain in P.N.G., snow

covered Mount Wilhelm. Then we landed on a small grass airstrip where about 150 natives were waiting. They loaded up our backpacks, put the food in their bilams, and we started up the mountains. And climbed up and up and up until I was sure we must have passed the moon and sun too. The villagers were peeking through the brush and climbing trees to see us. The girls would run their hands up and down my arms and feel my hair. I said to them, "Mi narapela kain meri, eh?" ("I'm a different kind of girl, eh?"), and they all busted out laughing. I was indeed another kind of girl than they had ever seen. The children hang back and stare with big eyes. We met a lapun meri (old woman) who screeched and crooned with toothless delight at our arrival. Another old man went off into an enraptured speech in Kumboi, "In 1975 we gained independence as a country. That year was the last time I saw a white man. Now I am happy to see white brothers and sisters."

It seems that the only way out of here is 3 hours walk down the mountain to the airstrip, and then to fly out. Most of the locals have never left these mountains. Pastor Allen and his wife Priscilla have given us their house. It is made with woven bark and grass and is the nicest hut I have stayed in. Pastor Allen took us up to the top of the mountain. From this spot we could see the ocean and Karkar island one direction, Mount Wilhelm in another, and all the way to Mount Hagin in the other. I think we can see about one third of P.N.G. from up here. Allen offered me the land at this highest spot to build a house and live there while I study Kumboi.

July 18, 1995

"He teacheth my hands to war, so that a bow of steel is broken by mine arms. Thou hast also given me the shield of thy salvation: and thy right hand hath holden me up, and thy gentleness hath made me great."
Psalm 18:34-35

The people here are begging me to stay. They have promised land, a house, and plenty of help. I think the biggest need is a Pidgin and Kumboi dyglot and some literacy work—perhaps a school where the children could learn to read.

July 19, 1995

"Thou hast enlarged my steps under me, that my feet did not slip."
Psalm 18:36

It is really very funny the way these verses fall on just the right day. This morning we got up early and began walking to the Aikram village—down, down, down the slippery mountain bush trails. My ankles and feet were twisting and flopping like rubber, my arms flailing like a windmill, but I somehow kept my balance as we crossed treacherous landslides, mountain rivers, and tangled roots. After two hours we arrived in the little Aikram village in which no other white people had ever been. The ancient wrinkled bubus (grandfathers) crooned and rocked back and forth as they thanked us for honoring their village. They took us to a hut where we can stay tonight and then escorted us around the village. Children with bellies bloated with worms followed us giggling.

July 20, 1995
"The Lord liveth; and blessed be my rock; and let the God of my salvation be exalted." Psalm 18:46
We had a really good day in the Aikram village. They taught me many new Kumboi words and laughed in delight every time I used one. Dirty black hands were continually feeling my braid, hands, and arms. Later I wiped the streaks of grime off of me. We walked to their gardens and watched the young men cut down a tree with a dull ax. Clearing land for a garden is a major job here. It is always on a mountainside, and the foliage is incredibly thick.

Last night, all the village leaders crowded into the small hut they had given us. Firelight gleamed on about 20 ancient, black faces. Dressed in loincloths, with an occasional shirt or shorts, they put National Geographic to shame. Long lengths of sugar cane were brought in, and they chewed and spat the clumps of white pulp into the fire pit. Pastor Allen began by telling them where I had come from, how I had gotten to this remote village, and what I wanted to do. They responded with enthusiasm. To have their own language down in writing!

On gnarled fingers, the old men counted off 16 villages and about 8 to 10,000 people that live in the neighboring valleys that speak Kumboi. I asked the old men, "If I come and spend half my life here working with your language, will you learn to read, or will I be wasting my time?" They were silent for a minute, then an old man spoke up, "This is a good question. Us old men and women cannot learn to read, we are too old. The younger ones, the children will learn. This will be good for them. Then they can come home and read to us old ones."

July 21, 1995

"Therefore will I give thanks unto thee, O LORD among the heathen, and sing praises unto thy name." Psalm 18:49

I am learning their names and faces. In fact, I even named one of them. A few days ago, some of the girls and I were sitting on a mat talking. I asked the name of one who was deaf. The other girls giggled and said that she doesn't have a name because she can't hear or speak correctly. She must have been in her mid-twenties and was very friendly. I said that I would give her a name, and they decided they also wanted new names. But I only named the deaf girl. I named her Leah and they have called her that ever since.

July 23, 1995

"The Heavens declare the glory of God; and the firmament sheweth his handiwork. Day unto day uttereth speech, and night unto night sheweth knowledge. There is no speech nor language where their voice is not heard." Psalm 19:1-3

I decided to try to translate a verse of scripture into Kumboi, to give Allen a better idea of translation and to give myself some more exposure to the language. So with an English Bible, lantern, pencil, and notepad, we proceeded to try to translate John 3:16. Allen was ambitious and thought it would take no more than a few minutes, but for the first hour, we couldn't get past the first phrase, "For God so loved." Allen couldn't think of the word for love. He would mutter one over and over and say, "No that's not right." Finally he said, "Simbiningi! That's the word. Write it down." And so I did. But today, with another language helper, I was going over a list of words, and when we came to the word for love, she gave me a totally different equivalent. So I read her the verse Allen and I had translated the night before and asked her if it was right. "Yes, that's right," she said, "For God so loved the world." "But you told me another word for love," I said. "What does simbiningi mean?" She looked confused and said, "It means love too." "Can you explain the difference?" I asked. She thought a minute and replied, "Simbiningi is when a mother looks at her child that is hurting and says, "I simbiningi you. I love you, I have compassion and mercy and pity, and I desire to change what is hurting you. This is the right word to use. You don't want to say that God had admiration and appreciation for the world so he gave his son. You want to say that he loved and pitied us, and out of mercy gave his only son. Simbiningi is this word." How fine the lines of translation!

July 24, 1995

"The law of the LORD is perfect, converting the soul: the testimony of the Lord is sure, making wise the simple."Psalm 19:7

It is Monday afternoon, our last day in the mountains. I expect I will return to this place to do my work. I am not sorry, it is a beautiful place. And yet, I am reminded once again that missionary work is not the romantic picture that it is so often painted to be. Most would-be missionaries envision themselves sitting in the sunshine with a Bible in their laps, crowds of happy black children pressing close to hear the teacher's story. They imagine men and women begging for Bibles and getting saved left and right. Would to God that it were so! How come they never tell you that tribal people are filthy and smell so bad that sometimes you have to run into the bush and vomit? That the children scream and run because they never saw a white face before? That the women look down on you because you can't cook and work like they do? That you dare not look a man in the face or even witness to him for fear that he will take it as a come-on and follow you home and rape you? How come they never warn you in the books that the fellow Christians you are depending on for encouragement don't even see you as a missionary, but rather as an encumbrance? How come they never mention the fleas, lice, rats, leaches, and flies? How come they don't tell you that more likely than not you will never see the fruit of your labor or reward on this earth? Every real missionary has at sometime prayed, "Father if it be possible, let this cup pass from me, nevertheless, not my will, but thine be done." From the human standpoint, it is not worth it. Indeed, it is crazy. It is what Paul called "faith."

"Therefore my beloved brethren, be ye stedfast, unmoveable, always abounding in the work of the Lord, forasmuch as ye know that your labor is not in vain in the Lord."

If I ever give up and go home, it will be because I have lost sight of this truth. It is not in vain.

July 25, 1995

Today we were to take the plane out of the jungle. Well, we got up and walked all the way down to Kenanj, only to discover that the plane wasn't coming on Tuesday after all. Hot and sweaty and tired, we stared at the empty runway and then back at the mountain that we had just descended. And that's Papua New Guinea for you. Three hours of climbing back up in the glaring sun didn't cause me to appreciate the scenery like I could have. Everyone cheered at having us back again. It seems to entertain them just watching Gabe and me. In this culture brothers and sisters ignore each other from an early age. Guys and girls don't make friends and talk with each other either. And it's up to the girls to do the proposing.

July 26, 1995

Last night it stormed like I have never seen before. I always sleep better in storms, but last night I could not sleep at all. The lightning kept our dark hut lit like daylight, and the thunder shook the ground every time it blasted. But at daybreak the sky was clear.

This morning we got up early and started hiking back down. When we arrived, they told us that the plane wasn't coming until this afternoon. So I am sitting on a rock overlooking the grass airstrip waiting for time to pass. It is hard to believe that our time is nearly over. Only three more days and we will be home. Everyone should take a trip like this just once. Every Christian ought to see places where the gospel has never been and feel the weight of responsibility.

Two hours left to wait for that crazy MAF pilot and plane.

Well, two hours passed and then two more. Three P.M., and no plane. Then the clouds began to roll in. Great gray masses poured into the valley and then it began to rain. Wet and muddy, we took shelter under a nearby hut. Squatting there in the dust, Gabe and I looked at each other disgustedly.

News came over the radio that the plane could not come today and would be here tomorrow morning. Meanwhile, we were wet and miserable and hungry, with darkness creeping up on us. So we started running, and ran about two miles in the rain to a vacant hut. That is where I am now. Someone built a fire, and I put on dry clothes while Gabe and Timothy walked back to the trade store and got some rice and sitko meat, or maybe I should say sicko meat. It was worse than cat food. A sickly paste made up of meat leftovers. Allen warmed it up and poured the gooey mess over some rice. If it wasn't for the fact that I haven't had a meal since noon the day before, I think I would have thrown up at the sight and smell of it. Give me live grub-worms any day. But we both ate it anyway. So tonight we are camping out in this hut hoping the plane will come in the morning.

July 27, 1995

"More to be desired are they than gold: sweeter also than the honey and the honeycomb."Psalm 19:10

Morning dawned bright and clear. Cheerful and only a little worse for the wear, we loaded up once again and trekked back to the air strip. News came that the airplane had been stranded at Simbai overnight because of weather conditions and would arrive shortly. It did, only to leave without us. It made two more flights before it returned for us.

July 29, 1995

It is still the 29th, and has been for the last two days. We are on our last flight toward home. Another hour and we will be seeing Mom and Dad at the gate. How quickly this trip has gone! It seems only a few days ago that we left for P.N.G.. Looking back, I can see God's hand on this trip and our lives in so many ways. It is the power of prayer, or rather the power of the God who answers prayer. Our meeting with the Lindseys in Port Moresby; Cathy Yalio and her decision to come with me; the Williamses in Madang; and Pastor Allen, the only witness among his people; those two weeks in the mountains and our safety over incredible trails; the village of Aikram and their willingness to accept me into their lives and homes; and then our safety on the way back despite all odds; also the presence of Bryan and Ingrid in Hong Kong and their help. There must be more answers to prayer that we are not even aware of. I'm so glad I serve the Living God!

This short chapter of my life has ended, and it's time to begin another. As Joshua piled up those stones in the Jordan River, I'll write down these things to record the faithfulness of my God.

One year later...
July 27, 1996

"Only fear the LORD, and serve him in truth with all your heart: for consider how great things he hath done for you." 1 Samuel 12:24

Five years ago I began to prepare for this day, the day I stepped on to a foreign shore and called it home for the gospel's sake. For five years I've been dreaming, planning, and praying toward this end. How many times have I stepped off the edge of safety and walked on sheer air because God led me there? Yet it never gets easier. Every time He says come and beckons me to walk where none have gone before, my knees tremble, my mouth goes dry, and I go forward with more fear than faith. This is by far the most dramatic step I've ever taken. If it weren't for that still, small voice, I'd fear I had lost my mind.

August 14, 1996

*"There shall not any man be able to stand before thee all the days of thy life:
as I was with Moses, so I will be with thee, I will not fail thee nor forsake
thee." Joshua 1:5*

I'm squatting here in an Aikram hut, every bone in my body hurts.
Yesterday we waited on the MAF [Missionary Aviation Fellowship] airplane until 2:00 P.M. Then we flew from airstrip to airstrip in the bush
until 4:00 P.M. There are so many places out here, little holes in the jungle
where filthy, half-dressed people survive from day to day and die without
ever hearing the gospel once. At every airstrip, I wanted to get out, stay
there, and learn the Bundi language, the Ganj, the Marung, or the Ti so
I could tell them about Jesus. We finally landed on the Kenanj airstrip
with all our supplies and roofing tin. I jumped from the plane, bursting
with excitement and searching the sea of faces for Pastor Allen or any of
the Fokefoke bunch. Not a recognizable soul in sight. They unloaded tin,
food, and personal belongings while I continued to gaze hopefully around
for somebody I knew. Somebody in the staring mob was a Christian and
guessed I must be the Bible translator that Pastor Allen was waiting for. He
introduced himself as Manson and disappeared again to find us a place to
stay for the night with a businessman who lived near the airstrip. We were
also able to store our stuff out of the soon-coming rain.

The next morning, four of them accompanied us all the way to Aikram.
We left everything but our sleeping bags at Kenanj. We took several short
cuts and never stopped to eat, and as a result made excellent time, arriving
in less than five hours. I've got a couple of walking blisters, but otherwise I
weathered the trip pretty well.

The reception at Aikram was enormous. For several miles before we
arrived, you could hear the women's singsong voices in the gardens far
below. They sang, "Yaow, yaowa awan Ai yande yaow, yaowa." (Yes, yes,
my sister come, yes, yes), as well as wordless trills like so many birds.
When two or three got going at once, it sounded pretty tropical. When
we finally did get to Aikram, we were mobbed, literally attacked. We were
hugged breathless and beaten on with a rhythm to match the loud welcoming chants. It must have sounded like a Pentecostal revival. Nathan meant
to film my welcome into the village, but it was impossible since he was
mobbed as well. Pastor Allen put it imply, "Unexpected, but very welcome." Tonight we sleep in a newly built hut for Pastor Allen in the Aikram
village, Asai valley, Madang province, Papua New Guinea. Thank you God
for getting us here at last.

August 15, 1996

"Only be strong and of a good courage, for unto this people shalt thou divide the land for an inheritance, which I sware unto their fathers to give to them."
Joshua 1:6

Already the village sounds have become familiar to my ears. The bird that sings three notes, Do, Ray, Me, like an opera singer warming up, the rooster that crows regardless of the hour, the crackling of fires, and the sing-song voices of the old women calling to each other. I got all our stuff packed into the room where I sleep. About 15 of the young people went down to Kenanj yesterday and brought it all up here. They had to break up the purple box; it was so heavy. The girls had a blast going through my belongings. The little flaxen-haired doll and my photo albums were big hits. We weren't missing anything though, and it must have been a grueling ten-hour hike. As soon as it was dark, Nathan and I went down to the water source and took turns bathing in the icy mountain water. It's cold enough here to wear a jacket in the evenings. The only thing that keeps one from getting pneumonia after being soaked in that cold water is that the hike back up to the village is so strenuous. By the time you reach your hut, you are sweating with effort. The paths to the toilet and the water are very tricky, and Nathan says that I use my "assets" to get down them.

As of this morning, I began cooking outside over a fire for Nathan and myself. Pinto beans seasoned with onions and garlic was my first experiment. Everyone in the village eventually came by to look and smell. Nathan began the day by building a table for me. Frank, Jerry and Dick helped, so I fed them beans too. We ate it all. The table was a big success. They cut the wood and dragged it out of the bush. It was done soon after lunch, and they began on a chair. That was finished by 3 P.M., and now I am seated on the chair writing at the table—all made with bush material, except for the nails. These guys are really good with their machetes, so Nathan gets them to prepare and notch the wood while he bosses how it's put together. They were very proud of the finished product.

I started language learning in earnest this afternoon. Rosinda, who speaks English as well, helped me with all the body parts. She is Pastor Allen's sister, and dedicated to helping me. The Kumboi language is very backed [a linguists term meaning from the rear of the throat] and nasal. When they pronounce it slowly, it is entirely different from normal speech. I am praying, along with the Aikram people, that I'll learn their tok ples [native language] quickly.

August 17, 1996

"This book of the law shall not depart out of thy mouth; but thou shalt meditate therein day and night, that thou mayest observe to do according to all that is written therein: for then thou shalt make thy way prosperous, and then thou shalt have good success." Joshua 1:8

Saturday afternoon.

Nathan built a bed and shelf, so both the food and I are up off the floor now. He and Frank are now making a cross-bow to kill cassowaries [big bird]. Yesterday I taught Frank three chords on the Uke, and he is determined to learn how to play. I also gave out all the bright colored scarves to the girls. Every now and then a brilliantly clad head bobs by my window.

Cooking outside was a bit harder yesterday because it rained on and off. The wood is wet and gives off a lot of smoke. Nathan suggested I get a pair of goggles and silk scarf to wear around my nose. I can just imagine me squatting in a cloud of smoke with goggles and scarf while I hold a frying pan over a smoking fire.

There's a bird here that keeps us laughing. Nathan calls it "the Shalom bird," after our sister. It sounds like it's having a nervous breakdown all the time.

Language lessons are going well. The old folks teach me the most. Somehow the words spoken with physical expression and context stick in my mind. "Aswan Ai yande," crooned by the old women, I always remember—"Come my sister." They taught me the response in the same sing song voice: "Aswin Ami yande, I'm coming my mother."

The Aikram village is a family. Everyone is related. The people that are saved are mostly all family. There are now 7 fellowships between here and Kenainj. Most are Kumboi; one is Ganj.

The understanding of the gospel seems somewhat subjective. They focus on human responsibility. The Pidgin word to describe salvation is, "Tainin bel na kamap Kristen, Turn your emotions/affections and come up/become a Christian." True, but not the whole truth. I've heard no mention of substitution or blood atonement. I know some of them are Christians, you can see the difference in their eyes. But a lot of them that have been placed in the Christian/Baptist category don't really understand the gospel. What can you expect in a church without the Bible? Outsiders are rarely saved unless they marry into the clan and convert. A sad state, I know, but the flip side of the coin shows that most, or all, of these people would be genuinely saved if they ever clearly heard the truth. I wish I were fluent in Kumboi, and a preacher! How sweet the book of Romans,

Hebrews, Ephesians, and John would be to preach to open and eager ears!
How glad I am to have the Bible with all its glorious truths in my heart
language.

August 18, 1996

"And as soon as we heard these things, our hearts did melt, neither did there
remain any more courage in any man, because of you: for the LORD your
God, he is God in heaven above, and in earth beneath." Joshua 2:11

Sunday afternoon.

I missed a day somewhere this week. I got up this morning thinking
it was Saturday. Services start at 8:30, underneath the little lean-to they
call Rock Baptist Church. The singing here badly needs help. There are no
words to describe it. Frank comes twice a day to practice on my Ukelele.
He learns chords quickly but sings along off key and with zero timing.
Frank will be my adopted brother when Nathan leaves. His sister Rosinda
is already my main language helper. The other day she told me that Leah,
the deaf girl I named last year, had moved back to her own village but
still came to visit sometimes. I told her that deaf people in the U.S. had a
language with their hands and showed her some signs. This amazed her and
the next day a whole group of girls cornered me, wanting to know more
about this hand language. In their minds, someone born deaf is simply
born without the ability to communicate and lives a sadly solitary life. The
idea of communicating with signs fascinated them. If only Leah could speak
with signs, she could understand the gospel.

The Kumboi language is starting to make a little more sense to my
ears. I began some practical expression learning yesterday and discovered
some verb patterns. The vowel in the verb must always match the person
marker. Yant aswin, is "I come." Nant aswan, is "you come." This rule carries
through with all the verbs I've encountered so far. Well, our first week
in the village has gone quickly. I've learned a lot but still feel like a pink
flamingo in a flock of crows. I'm so glad to have Nathan here. It's nice to
have someone around that can laugh at your jokes and tell some that you
understand. We wrote down the things that we learned this week.

THiNGs We lEArnEd oUr FiRSt wEeK iN tHe VILLagE.

#1: That duct tape is a product of Divine creation, not human
invention.

#2: That an outhouse is a haven of blessed privacy (if it weren't
for the flies, I'd live in one.)

#3: That America has come a long way since Babel, while others haven't progressed at all.

#4: That when you stop smelling your neighbors, it's time to take a bath.

#5: That it's wise to take your bath after dark because your new friends aren't immoral, just curious to know if you're white all over.

#6: That the woman screaming hysterically in the bush is really just an insect's mating call.

#7: That brown rice can be eaten three times a day, seven days a week.

#8: That smoke follows beauty and anything else that tries squatting close enough to the fire to cook.

And we're still learning. That's just the first week.

August 19, 1996

"And they said unto Joshua, Truly the LORD hath delivered into our hands all the land; for even all the inhabitants of the country do faint because of us." Joshua 2:24

Monday afternoon.

I'm working on my last battery here and I hope the power holds out long enough to finish. It has been too cloudy today to charge my computer or the camcorder batteries. The Aikram folks are still working on clearing the land where my house is going to sit. They've just about got it done. The man that owns the bush sawmill is supposed to return today, and we're going to see him about cutting some crude lumber for us. Time is going by so quickly.

Nathan is at loose ends right now. He dug a better path down to the outhouse and worked on the one to the water, but there's not much he can do until the land is ready to build on and the timber cut. We have been memorizing two verses a day from Hebrews chapter eleven. We are now working on the passage about Abraham and enjoying it very much. In the evenings we take turns reading four chapters out of the Bible, then work on memorization, and finally talk about what needs to be prayed for, and then take turns praying. It is one of the best parts of the day.

Pastor Allen is about to drive us both crazy. I don't know if it is insecurity or what, but he is continually apologizing for the living conditions and making plans for a bigger and better kingdom (if we have the money). That is simply P.N.G. culture. I've started just giving a vague smile and going on about my business. It must be hard for him to live up here with a whole lot less than he could have if he went back to his old job in town. It's totally against P.N.G. culture to go backwards like that. In fact, it's just plain retarded in their way of thinking. I guess he's got more guts than we give him credit for. Well, I've got a dirty bean pot to clean, so I'd better go now.

August 20, 1996
"And that all the people of the earth might know the hand of the LORD, that it is mighty: that ye might fear the LORD your God forever."
Joshua 4:24

Leah came by last night. She had no way of knowing that I was here, so it took her by surprise. She squealed with delight and shook her wrists, hands limp, in the Kumboi manner that expresses delight. She pointed to her village, (a day's walk) then to herself, and then gestured at Aikram and back toward her village to show me that she had been away and was on her way back home. Then she ran off and came back with an older lady and a young girl. I found out through Pidgin and Kumboi that this was her mother and sister. I gave her a small hand mirror and she waved goodbye, mouthing the word Amjipin, "I go." Then Jenny came with my guitar and photo album. She had gone all the way to Kenang to get them. I think it was the photo album that induced her to go all that way. Frank is sitting on the floor looking at it now. They love pictures. They appreciate the guitar too. So do I. I'm so glad I brought it. Nathan and I fought over it all evening.

Every night we brew up a big pot of tea and sip it while we read, sing and memorize scripture. After consuming about a quart of tea each, we have to get up a dozen times at night and go out. Last night it was raining and Nathan decided to try and hold it. Just as I was drifting off to sleep, I heard him mutter over in his room, "I feel like the Indian that drank too much tea before he went to bed." "How's that?" I asked. "He woke up the next morning in his teapee." Nathan's jokes have a special quality about them that I can't quite figure out.

Today he built two more shelves. One holds the books and one holds the dishes. This emptied the big purple box that all my books were packed in, so we filled it with water. I made another shelf for my computer in the corner. It looks rather incongruous sitting up on a hand-hewn shelf against woven pitpit walls.

My language helper went to the gardens today, so I worked on memorizing my first dialogue and some practical expressions. The most helpful phrase I've learned so far is, Nant tap a yimbe apan sak? "What do you call this thing?" Or, "How do you say…?"

There was a huge turnout to work on my house site. Another day's work and it will be all cleared and level. It's amazing what they can do with shovels. The four, old men, the saved fathers of the tribe, are real characters. Bil, Tombi, Jeshun, and Ben are their names. They work continually and keep my fire going for me. I can't pay them all for helping me, and they don't expect it, but I think what I'll do is buy enough lamb chops and rice for a huge feast and invite everybody that helps to build my house. They love mumus. It's their idea of a real party. Pastor Allen thinks it's a good idea too. Well, it is about to storm big-time and any cooking I want to do before night must be done now. It rains almost every evening and night during dry season. I wonder what it will be like in rainy season?

August 22, 1996
"Now faith is the substance of things hoped for, the evidence of things not seen." Hebrews 11:1

I always thought that if I was blind and had a seeing-eye dog that I'd name it faith, since we're supposed to walk by faith and not by sight. Nathan and I have made it all the way to verse 14 in Hebrews chapter eleven. Having someone to memorize with is fun. And being in a place where people don't have a Bible that they can read and fully understand the depth of its meaning causes me to appreciate the Word of God in my own language. Hebrews is so beautifully written. Every word, every phrase is rich with meaning and so perfectly said. What a privilege it is to be able to memorize and meditate on the very words of God.

This is Thursday morning. They are finishing digging off my house site today. There are about twelve men working and a few boys. Tomorrow morning Nathan and Allen are going up to look at the sawmill and see if Nathan can fix it. If he can, we'll get our lumber sawed there next week. Because Gabriel fixed it last year, and because the owner of the mill is Pastor Allen's uncle, and the trees belong to Allen, if Nathan fixes the sawmill again this time, we will get a very cheap price.

We have a little over two weeks left here in the village before we are supposed to go back to Madang. Allen plans on going with us. We now have a better idea of what we need to buy, and are making lists of tools, food, and miscellaneous items to get during the week we are back in town. I am hoping and praying that my crates will arrive safely and on time while we are there so I can fly them back with us. It is a strange feeling to be so isolated that there is no way of knowing or finding out how your family and friends are and what is going on in the outside world. It is like standing in the dark with your eyes wide open and still seeing nothing. So far we have been in excellent physical health. I know it is because of the folks at home praying for us. The people are cleaner than they were last year, I guess because they live closer to water now, but there is still a lot of filth. They wash their whole bodies about once a week, some more often than that, but they don't seem to wash their hands in between time. They scrub their pots until there is no black on them and scrub their clothes until they make holes in them, but they never seem to notice their faces, hands, and hair.

Talking about hair, the girls asked me yesterday if I had a secret potion that makes hair grow long. I told them the secret was washing and comb-ing it often and keeping it braided neatly. Their method of lice control is interesting. The younger children are simply shaved if they are found farm-ing lice. The others sit in rows and each one checks the head of the one in front of her, their fingers moving with a practiced rhythm. As a result of this daily inspection, they seem to stay fairly lice free. Just in case, I always rinse my hair with vinegar and comb it out with a fine tooth comb. We are adjusting quickly to bush life.

August 23, 1996

"These all died in faith, not having received the promises, but having seen them afar off, and were persuaded of them, and embraced them, and confessed that they were strangers and pilgrims on the earth. For they that say such things declare plainly that they seek a country. And truly, if they had been mindful of that country from whence they came out, they might have had opportunity to have returned." Hebrews 11: 13-15

I was thinking yesterday morning about what is the hardest thing to endure on the mission field. I went over all the physical hardships and dangers, sacrifices in food and comfort. I meditated on the loneliness and responsibilities that weigh you down. Although none of these are to be cast aside as insignificant, they are none of them any worse than the oth-ers to bear. So, what is the hardest thing to take in stride out here in the bush? It's an age-old trial, a testing as old as Abraham, and a hardship that glorifies God more than any other; it's walking by faith. It is living day-in and day-out not knowing if you are wasting your time, wondering if you are doing any good. It is the fear that it was only your emotions that called you here, not that still small voice. It is wishing, continually, that you knew the end of the story and could be sure that you really are doing something worthwhile and aren't suffering for no reason at all. It is seeing the admiring looks on the faces of pastors, friends, and fellow missionaries that say "how brave you are, we appreciate your courage and God does too." And yet, it never occurs to them that God might be planning to do something incredible, work miracles and save souls. They see Him as playing games with me, growing me up, changing me, preparing me to be the paragon Christian example for all the young folks at home. I hope He does change and purify me, I surely need it, but couldn't He possibly mean business enough to use me while He's at it? I couldn't continue here if I thought all God was interested in was growing me up. And yet when nine out of ten people seem to see that as the end of all ministry—personal growth and spiritual arrival—I get to wondering that maybe God really isn't going to work any miracles and do marvelous things with me—as well as to me. It is a faithless, self-centered thought, and I'm ashamed to admit that it runs through my mind far too often. God's love and attention is not limited. He so loved the world—the whole world. He is not willing that any should perish—not any at all. I know that He will use me as much as He possibly can, as much as I will let Him, to reach as many people as possible in my lifetime. Oh, He'll grow me up while He's at it. But that is just a side benefit, an extra blessing that overflows off the top of everything else He's going to do. God intends to glorify Himself and to make Himself known to as many people on earth as He can, and if I'm willing to help in that mission, you better believe He's going to use me, and anybody else that puts themselves in His hands. Amen. I should have been a Methodist.

What brought all this to mind was something Pastor Allen said yesterday. After they finished digging the foundation for my house site, they all went over to the komp kurip, kitchen house, to make and eat a big mumu. We joined them and sat outside telling stories and eating baked kanyim, bananas. Pastor Allen said thoughtfully, "What if I had not flown to town that Monday last year when you were walking in the market? Where would you be now? Would we have ever gotten a missionary to come learn our tok ples and translate a Bible for us? What if I had not heard the gospel in 1983 and gotten saved? My people and I would all be lost and on our way to Hell. Did you ever wonder these things, Sister Rebekah?" I admitted that I had, but that it was obvious that God was interested in the Kumboi people and that His hand was leading. He agreed somberly, "Yes, God is big, and God is in control."

Then he began to recall the last couple decades and the grace of God in his life. "My tambunas (ancestors) were well known and had a reputation for being tough and fighters. We never lost our land and could always get any woman we wanted. The seven fathers were feared and respected by all the surrounding peoples. I was born to the eldest brother of our seven fathers and became the leader and inherited all the land. I was proud and no good just like my fathers. Then I went to town and heard the gospel from a missionary. I believed that Jesus died for me and I got saved. I went to Bible school and in '87 came back to my land and my people. I was afraid that they would be angry and fight if I witnessed to them but I went first to my father and told him that I was now a Christian and could no longer live the way I had before. I witnessed to him and he got saved. Then my brothers and sisters. Then I went to the next father (uncle) and after a while he and his family all believed and became Christians. Others were angry. They came in the night with their axes and bows and arrows. They chopped up the gardens and houses and they held their axes over me and said they were going to kill me. I reminded them of the reputation of my clan and that we had always been respected and feared. I told them that I could fight just like them but that Jesus had saved me and I was now willing to die for the gospel because it was the truth, so they could just go ahead and kill me, I would not resist. They became afraid and ran away. Now four of my fathers have believed and they and their families have ceased from the haiden (heathen) ways and follow Christ. Others came and heard the gospel as well. It has been nine years now. There are seven different fellowships started in different villages in these mountains. One in the Ganj area and six in the Kumboi. We are praying for the three unsaved fathers and their families as well as all the other Kumboi that have not yet believed." I was awed and humbled at the grace of God shown here in the regions beyond, as well as encouraged and given confidence in the continuing work of the Lord here among them. My God can do anything. Not having received the promises, yet I can see them afar off, and I'm persuaded of them. Because He that promised is definitely faithful.

August 24, 1996
"But now they desire a better country, that is, an heavenly: wherefore God is not ashamed to be called their God: for he hath prepared for them a city."
Hebrews 11:16

This is Saturday afternoon. Yesterday Nathan went to have a look at the sawmill and see if he could fix it. He worked on some fuel filters and replaced the tank, but still has to go back Monday to clean out the carburetor. They had to go all the way to Kongoro to pick up some parts and spent about half the day just walking. Hopefully we might even get the lumber free. It is a primitive set up and may take two weeks to cut the wood we need for framing a simple 24 by 24-foot house.

Priscilla went to Kongoro Friday to visit some people, and got sick while she was there. A relapse of Malaria, plus she has some female problems as well. The best I could understand, when she was in Madang, in the hospital, this spring, they thought she might die, and had planned to do a hysterectomy. However because of the shortage of funds, and because the medicine seemed to work, they sent her home without surgery and a warning to take it easy. She still gets ill occasionally, and I'm worried Allen might lose her yet. Anyway, Allen went to join her in Kongoro until Sunday afternoon. The carpenter that he had visiting from Madang got himself a girlfriend and is living in adultery with her right in their house. Allen told the girl to leave, and she would not. He hasn't got the money to send the guy back to Madang and the Aikram people are pretty upset with the situation. Nathan and I prayed about it and decided to buy his plane ticket out of here Monday. We could have used his tools and expertise in bush building, but it is probably best to run him off under the circumstances. Eighty-four kina is the price of a one way ticket. Pastor Allen was greatly relieved to hear of our decision. He has really gotten himself in a tight spot this time. Well, my battery is running low, so I've got to sign off and save this. Besides, a big rain is coming and there are things to be done before it gets here.

August 25, 1996

"Hast thou not known? Hast thou not heard, that the everlasting God, the LORD, the Creator of the ends of the earth, fainteth not, neither is weary? There is no searching of his understanding." Isaiah 40:28

I must write quickly, as night is falling and my battery is low. Nathan has gone with the guys to Fogefoge for the night and will work on the sawmill tomorrow morning, returning here in the afternoon. Pastor Allen and his wife just returned. Priscilla is still sick. We had an interesting day. We sang a special for church this morning and spent the afternoon loafing with our Kumboi friends. Nathan and the guys staked out the house and squared everything up for the posts. Rosinda was gone this afternoon, so I was stuck without anyone that knew even a smattering of English. As a result, I made great leaps and bounds in my Pidgin and tok ples learning. Anna, Jenny, Nataline, and Rosilla sat under the house with me and we talked about everything from maternity tops to ozone layers—all in Pidgin. Who knows what they thought we were talking about? One of the fathers came by, Tombi, and pointed at my solar light, stuck on a post outside our house. "Computer," he said beaming, proud of his English word. He must have heard that I have a computer and assumed that this unidentifiable object was the mysterious modern machine everyone was talking about.

I gave away a small sack full of satin underwear to all the girls this afternoon. You never heard such squeals of delight. Then I brought out the small blonde doll that I had packed as a last minute thought. Equal delight. They passed it around, oooing over the flaxen hair and blue eyes. One lady pulled out her breast and pretended to nurse it, sending everybody into shrieks of hilarious laughter. Her own little boy, sitting in her lap, started to wail in terror and bat it away. We had a good time to say the least. They examined my hair, nails, freckles, sunburn, etc. and discussed every part of me with great interest. Tomorrow is the beginning of our third week here. Em tasol.

August 28, 1996

"He giveth power to the faint; and to them that have no might he increaseth strength." Isaiah 40:29

It has been impossible to write for the last two days because of the rain. Today is cloudy as well, but enough sun to charge my computer battery. Nathan is gone to the sawmill with everybody else from Aikram. He, or should I say, God, fixed the sawmill Monday. They are going to move it today and hopefully start cutting. The owner is going to charge us 500 kina ($400.00) to cut all the timber for my house, another two rooms on Pastor Allen's house and extra to use for whatever we need it for. It is not as cheap as we had hoped to get it, but still not bad. I will have a much more secure and permanent house than we had planned on, which is a great blessing. The walls will still be woven pitpit, but the roof will be tin, and I will actually have a floor! A real board floor.

Pastor Allen sent the carpenter's girlfriend home and decided to keep him here until my house is built. I haven't decided what I think about his ethics yet. I spent all morning down at the water, washing our dirty clothes for the past week. Washing clothes is a major chore here. Just getting to the water is a good day's work, then you have to wash each separate piece of clothing with a bar of soap under the icy flow of water, and clothes get really dirty here. By the time you make it back up to the top of the trail, you're covered with mud, head to toe. You know you're in the bush when it takes mud boots, umbrella, and flashlight to go to the bathroom or to go get a drink of water. Thankfully, they do plan on improving the trail; I don't know if that means a ski lift or a helicopter, but I'm looking forward to it.

I think I know just about everybody in the Aikram Christian family by name now. I think I'll describe a few of the most unique characters here. The one that catches my interest most is Waina. She is the wife of Father Jashun, about forty-five years old. She must have been a great beauty in her day, and is still a regal figure in her own right. There is something about her countenance that makes you feel glad all over. She is tall, and walks with a light, dancing step that comes from years of carrying burdens on her head and having to keep balance with her waist rather than shoulders, lest she spill what she is carrying. She looks just like Katherine Hepburn when she smiles, tilting her head back and to the right, showing all her teeth and half closing her eyes in a manner that says clearly, it's a wonderful world. Waina is one of the strongest Christian mothers in the Church here, and everybody loves her. Then there is Wimung, a boy about 10 years old. His shorts are always on the verge of dropping below his knees, and the only thing left of his shirt is the collar, which he faithfully wears. You hear his name hollered continually throughout the day, he's everyone's errand boy. He is cheerful, and adores Nathan.

Then there is Anna, Waina's daughter. She is about 14 years old and the typical teenage girl. She talks a blue streak and is never still. Anna is extremely intelligent, but never had the chance to go to school. She has taught herself how to read Pidgin and is singing every time I see her.

Jerry is Allen's younger brother and his wife's name is Nataline. They are a precious couple with three young children. Jerry is Pastor Allen's right hand man and I suspect he does carry 50% of the ministry in a quiet, background manner. He is a very hard worker and always busy. I hope to use him in translation.

Lawrence is a cousin of Pastor Allen's and about 32 years old. He is a commanding figure, but oddly enough though, he is very shy and you never see him around. Lawrence studies a great deal and is hungry to know as much as he can about the Bible and it's truths. He preaches every other Sunday. I hope to use him in translation as well.

Jenny is the oldest single girl here, about 26 years old, I'd guess. She speaks only Kumboi and a little Pidgin. Jenny never had any schooling either and has never been outside of these mountains. She taught herself to read Pidgin out of the Pidgin Bible by memorizing verses. She is a sweet girl.

Rosinda is her younger sister and, at the time, my language helper. Rosinda did go out to Madang and go to school up to the 10th grade. She speaks some English and is very sharp. She is quiet and seems to be the leader of all the young females around. I doubt she will stay here in the mountains.

Frank is her brother and Nathan's buddy. Frank also went to school and can read and write well. He speaks some English and wants to continue his schooling somewhere, somehow and be a teacher.

The Fathers are all very interesting characters, but I haven't gotten to know them very well because they don't speak any English and not much Pidgin, and I haven't learned their language yet.

Priscilla, Pastor Allen's wife, is a jewel. I doubt he would stay here if it wasn't for her. She is eternally minded in a way that is against P.N.G. culture. When something of value is lost or broken, she says, "Never mind, I wasn't going to take it to Heaven with me anyway." When Pastor Allen gets discouraged and starts complaining about the lack of physical comforts and the frustrations of ministry, she smiles cheerfully and sings, "Little is much when God is in it; Labor not for wealth or fame; There's a crown and you can win it, if you go in Jesus' name." She respects and admires him to such a degree that it spurs him on to keep trying. But Priscilla is continually ill, and I'm afraid she won't live to be very old. She needs a lot of prayer. All of these people need a lot of prayer. They will be the first Kumboi people to get the word of God in their own language, and will be the ones responsible for teaching their own how to read, and taking the word to all the other villages around.

August 31, 1996

"Be careful for nothing; but in everything by prayer and supplication with thanksgiving let your request be made known unto God." Philippians 4:6

Saturday morning.

Everyone is resting today. Thursday they cut down a big tree and cut it into logs. Friday they carried the sawmill down and set it up and cut for about two hours. Monday they are supposed to start cutting in earnest. Nathan is about to climb the walls in frustration at the way they do things here. Every job has to be done together, and they simply cannot work on two projects at the same time. If one person is sharpening the chain saw, the rest sit and watch until he's done before they start clearing brush or moving the sawmill. And only one project a day can be done. If they finish cutting the tree down at 1:00 P.M. they go home and come back the next day to cut it up. It is humorous at first, but frustrating after a while. It's no wonder they haven't progressed beyond primitive bush life. Nathan said

what was coming to be a habit, "If you cracked a P.N.G.'s head open, you'd
find a piece of kawkaw wrapped in greens." Different cultures.

I spent yesterday working on separating and uniting procedures, trying
to discover what the Kumboi alphabet is. The vowels are giving me problems. The shwa is used in probably 60% of their words, and I don't have
a symbol for it on my keyboard. I would use / i / instead except I need
that for the / i / phoneme. I also need an epsilon and the / e / but since
the 'aye' sound only occurs every now and then, I will write it as (ey). The
other vowels are / o /, / u /, / ^ /, as well as the vowel clusters, au, ai,
and oi. There is the possibility of writing the Eee sound as (iy) and the
using the / i / symbol for the schwa. I'm still working on it. Lyle Shultz,
translator for the neighboring language that is 70% cognate, solved the
problem by simply using the absence of a vowel for the shwa. But that
left the majority of their words written like ancient Hebrew. Minmin,
the word for happiness, was written, mnmn. The word for compassion,
simbiningi, was written smbngni. The people were not pleased with the
way it looked and complained that it was not a language—therefore, did
not learn to read it.

I would like Kumboi to be written with as similar an alphabet to Pidgin
as possible, since that is what they are used to. There is also a silent /L/
that is made with the tongue stationed on the alveolar ridge while air is
blown around it noisely. It only occurs every now and then and I'm not
sure what to do with it yet. I've only been here three weeks; maybe I
should take it a little slower. I wish my crates were here so I could use my
tapes to record my language helper and practice pronunciation.

Nathan and I are getting tired of the monotony of our diet. Rice for
breakfast, rice and tin meat and onions for lunch, and either leftover rice
or ramen for supper. Em tasol. Next time I buy groceries, I'm going to try
for more variety. This morning I tried frying some bananas for breakfast. It
worked all right, but you get smoked trying to hover around the fire while
they fry. One more week before we go back to town. It turned out that we
bought the exact amount of food to last to the day we leave. Nothing extra.
I didn't figure it that close, I guess God did.

Pastor Allen is determined to go with us to Madang, but I can't think of
a reason for him to go. It will cost me a hundred kina to get him there and
back, and I was sort of looking forward to a break from his overwhelming
company. I think I'll tell him that we really need him to stay here since the
sawmill won't be done cutting our lumber and the people need to start
weaving the pitpit and cutting the pandanus wood for the outside of the

house. I hope he won't think we are mad at him. In this culture, if you try to avoid someone's presence, you are angry with them. Kumboi people stay together at all times, no one does anything alone, whether it's taking a walk or taking a bath. Hard for me to get used to, to say the least. Thankfully, they realize we are different and give us a little space, all the while apologizing for not keeping us company.

September 4, 1996

"Hear my cry, O God; attend unto my prayer. From the end of the earth will I cry unto thee, when my heart is overwhelmed: lead me to the rock that is higher than I." Psalm 61:1-2

I put music to these verses the other day. If this isn't the end of the earth, I don't know where the end is. Old Bil, the father of Allen, asked Nathan if there were people beyond the land where we come from, or if we lived on the end of the world. I guess he thinks the world is flat.

This is Wednesday afternoon, I have been remiss in keeping diary. The sawmill crew has been going full time since Monday, although it rained all day yesterday. Nathan hasn't had anything to do, so he just hangs around the house bugging me and I don't get anything done either. Today he went to Kenanj with Frank to radio MAF Madang and ask them to call Jerry Williamses and tell him to put two and three-inch nails on the next plane out this direction. They plan to start building tomorrow. The carpenter that is up here visiting Pastor Allen will be the head man in charge. He appears to be one of the best in Madang. The house will consist of one 17x12 room for kitchen and living room, one 8x12 room for Cathy, one 10x12 room for my office and bedroom, one 6x12 room as storage and a 7x12 foot porch complete with firepit. It will be up off the ground on poles about 4 or 5 feet.

Nathan and I planted a garden yesterday, down in the hollow behind where the house will sit. It is made up of small raised beds. We planted lettuce, cabbage, radishes, carrots, swiss chard, kale, and onions. When we get to Madang again I'm going to look for garlic plants, tomato plants and some corn seed. The soil is incredibly rich and black. The avocado plants grow and produce within two years, and the fruit is huge. I hope to plant some avocado plants around the house as well.

After thinking, and even dreaming about the consonant and vowel symbol problem, I got out my Microsoft Word book and my Publishers book and skim read both for any information on alternative keyboards and symbols and characters. There was one small sentence in the Microsoft Word book that mentioned symbols and I followed the trail. It took several hours and there were no directions in Help (that I could find) on how to actually change the keyboard or add extra symbols, but I did find the symbols I needed and after a while managed to assign a name to each one. For example: Ctrl + g is the password key for /(/ and Ctrl + z for /(/. This slows typing speed down a little, but nothing to complain about. I've also been studying Lyle Sholtz's dictionary and ethnologue on the Kalam language. It discouraged me a little; it was so overwhelming. This is no easy language I have tackled. I shouldn't have read the last chapter of the book and tried to imagine everything in between. One step at a time.

Yesterday we made tortillas with some flour Allen brought back from Kenanj. They were much enjoyed. Later I made chocolate pudding, and that was a success as well. There are a lot of things you can do with plain white flour and powdered milk. I wish they had powdered eggs in P.N.G.. Well, that brings me up to date. We have four more days before we head back to Madang for supplies. I hope and pray my crates make it to Madang while we are there.

September 6, 1996
"For God is not unrighteous to forget your work and labour of love, which ye have showed toward his name, in that ye have ministered to the saints, and do minister." Hebrews 6:10

Nathan and I finished memorizing Hebrews chapter eleven last night. We plan to start on chapter four tomorrow. This is Saturday and we will be leaving for Madang tomorrow after the service, staying in Kenanj overnight in case the plane decides to come early for a change.

Rainy season has started. It has rained every day this week. The guys working at the sawmill managed to finish cutting the tree up any way. They celebrated yesterday by cooking four bags of rice that we provided and having a feast. The sawmill owner took one look at all the lumber cut and said he wanted more money. "No more money, no more lumber." My first inclination was to tell him that we'll keep our money and buy lumber from somebody that keeps their word, then light the pile of lumber and let it burn. But that is just pride, and so we have said nothing so far, except to God. He, Awong, is coming by for his 500 kina tomorrow. I'm going to write up a receipt for him to sign, agreeing that we get all the lumber we need to build a house—the original agreement. Meanwhile we are praying that he will cooperate.

The Aikram folks plan to carry down the rest of the wood and start building while we are in Madang. I hope Nathan can get his visa extended so he can return and build my shelves. I'd rather have shelves than a house.

Meanwhile, language learning goes on at a little slower pace than before. I discovered that the ever-present shwa vowel that has been giving me grief is a consonant release vowel (at least most of the time). In other words, some consonants must be released with a vowel. Example: the English words cress and prayed would be pronounced like the English words caress and parade by a Kumboi speaker. There are no consonant clusters. Wycliff decided that the sister dialect had many words that were really voweless. Being composed of consonants with vowel releases. That's why Lyle Sholtz wrote Kalam without the vowel shwa and why the Kalam words look so strange, since 60% or more are shwa words. So what shall I do with it now? I haven't figured that one out yet. My language helper has been busy all week, so I have only been able to study what she has already given me and read the dictionary and ethnologue produced by Wycliff on the neighboring dialect. The old people are doing their best to help me learn their language, since they don't speak any Pidgin and we have no other way to communicate. The other day, Tombi came to the door with his hands full of white potatoes (I told them that white meris eat white potatoes) I forgot to speak in tok ples, and said in English, "Thank you!" He beamed at me and replied, "Thank you!" I laughed and said automatically, "No, you're welcome." He nodded and said as he turned to go; "No, you're welcome." Ah well, I'm here to learn their language, not teach them mine. Well, until we reach Madang...

September 12, 1996
"Wherefore holy brethren, partakers of the heavenly calling, consider the Apostle and High Priest of our profession, Christ Jesus." Hebrews 3:1

Reculturalization! How nice it is to be back in Madang. So much has happened that I'd better start at the beginning. Sunday, Awong was supposed to come by and sign a receipt I wrote up stating that he gets 500 kina and I get all the wood to build a house. He never came and we finally left for Kenainj. The girls and Jerry and his wife accompanied us down on the hike. They took some terrible detours that were straight up, and by any standards I should have been dead with fatigue by the time we reached the airstrip that evening. But I had a strength I've never had before and made it just fine. There must have been an angel half carrying me all the way.

At the airstrip, we again stayed with the business man, Septimas Sasu, an unsaved relative of Pastor Allen. He has offered us the use of his house any time we need to fly in or out. What a blessing! The plane was supposed to come at 6:00 A.M. Monday morning. Nathan and I were squatting

obediently out on the airstrip all by ourselves at 6:00. The others started
trickling in a half hour later, amazed that we had come so early. You see,
if they say six in P.N.G., they really mean the 12-hour period between
6:00 A.M. and 6:00 P.M. So we waited until about eight, and the MAF
agent, David, called into Madang to find out when they were coming. "Oh,
they're coming soon but they can't take any passengers because they're going back to Hagen and not to Madang." "But we have a prearranged flight,
confirmed three times!" "Sorry, lady, the coffee's gotta go to Hagen. Stick
around, maybe Island Airways will come by today."

I looked around at the sea of black faces that could each stare, without
blinking, interminable lengths of time. "God knows what's going on," said
Nathan, "but I bet if you cracked a P.N.g. head open you'd find a piece of
kawkaw wrapped in greens." We found plenty more to say about them in
the next five hours. Everywhere we went, they followed, staring as hard as
they could. Nathan had to go to the bathroom (that phrase doesn't exactly
fit) and started hiking down the road to find a private bush. Of course a
bunch followed him. "Yu go we?" they asked him. "I need to use a toilet,"
Nathan growled exasperated. "O, just go in bush." They continued to ac-
company him, and when a group was passed on the road, "Wait man laik
i go toilet." So the company thereof was great and added to daily. "This
a good place," they advised him, and stood by waiting for the outcome.
Nathan took a look at the curious, expectant faces and said, "Never mind,
I'm going back." Now they were puzzled and the message to everyone that
passed was, "Wait man laik i go toilet, but find no satisfaction."

Back at the airstrip I wasn't too happy either. A sane human being can
take being stared at for quite a while, but after about three hours of being
an object of great fear and curiosity, you get pretty tired of mothers haul-
ing wimpering children up to look at the white meri and stare for a few
hours. Finally, thank God, it started raining. And I was the only one with
an umbrella. They huddled in the house behind us and stayed crowded in
the doorway, all of them straining to keep an eye on me. So I took a stroll
down the runway and out of sight. A few were curious enough to run out
in the rain to see what I was doing, but not for long. So I sat in the middle
of the wet runway in the rain while the bugs enjoyed an unexpected snack.
I was shamefully short on faith and thanksgiving. And yet God was good. I
should never doubt in the darkness what I have seen in the light, but somehow I always do.

Soon the sky cleared and MAF landed. I was seated on top an old oil
barrel in the middle of all the natives, the girls from Aikram leaning against

me in a friendly manner when the pilot climbed out of his plane. He'd never seen me before and looked like he couldn't believe his eyes. "How long have you been in here," he asked, "where are you staying?" I told him I was staying in a village a five-hour hike into the bush from the runway. He looked me over with cautious concern and asked, "Are you all right?" I was tempted to look blank and let my mouth hang slack while muttering incoherently, "Kawkaw, kawkaw," but instead I just assured him that I was quite sane and healthy.

Nathan asked if they would please take us to Madang and they said of course they were going to, didn't we have a prior arrangement with them? They just had to go to Hagen first and drop off the coffee and put us on a smaller plane, but if we were in a hurry they'd take us straight there and leave the coffee. Relief. Never doubt in the darkness what you've seen in the light. So we were off and also were able to arrange to charter a flight to Kenanj on Monday that will carry everything the plane can hold of our supplies and us.

We got to Madang around 3:30 and Jerry Williams came to pick us up and take us to the guesthouse. I took two showers, one after another, and Nathan did too. Marilyn Williams had planned a big meal for our return: roast beef, mashed potatoes and gravy, fresh vegetables, and finally, banana splits to top it all off. Did we ever eat! Being able to talk and laugh with people of our same language and culture was the best of all. The next morning, we sat down and went over our supply list. Two things that I didn't get tired of and really enjoyed in Aikram were canned chicken\ turkey meat and also the boxed cheddar cheese. It was real and tasted so good. The meat was only sold in one store, at three kina per can. They hadn't had very much of it, and the cheese was also in shortage at 2.50 a box. We have been praying that God would provide these two items in town, not really believing that he would. When we walked to town yesterday and to the grocery store, there were 75 boxes of cheese just in from Lae, during a cheese shortage. At the next grocery store there was a basket full of chicken turkey\meat reduced to 1.99 a can—five months supply. Was God laughing? To see Him answer small requests like that humbles me more than the greatest miracles. Can He really care that much? Well, today is Wednesday and we've much to do.

September 13, 1996

"Now unto him that is able to do exceedingly abundantly above all that we ask or think, according to the power that worketh in us, Unto him be glory in the church by Christ Jesus throughout all ages, world without end. Amen." Ephesians 3:20,21

Today is Shoshanna's birthday. She is thirteen years old, and she is the baby of the family. That makes me an old lady. I'm beginning to feel like one anyway. This is Friday and we have a lot of shopping to do. I made up a list of all the food supplies I should need for four months and took it to Anderson's grocery, the store with the biggest variety, and asked them if they could fill the order every four months and deliver it to the MAF hangar for me. Yes, they can and the food would be sold to me at wholesale prices since I'm buying huge cartons of many things and they don't have the overhead to worry about. So that cut out 60% of this week's shopping and worries. There are a lot of other supplies that I need this month that I won't ever need again: shovel, water barrels, rat traps, machete, etc. The business folks in this town know us now since we've been in every store every day and bought stuff that only bush people buy. They are very curious, and everyone asks where we are staying. I think I will come out to town every three or four months from now on and hire a plane to take me and my stuff to Kenanj all at once. There I'll hire the Simbai truck to come and pick everything up and take it to the bush trail junction (if the road isn't washed out) where the Aikram people can come and carry it all the way, since it's only a 50 minute walk from there. This would save a lot of time, work, and money if I can get everyone to cooperate. MAF and the grocery store are agreeable. The truck will be the catch, if there is any. Cathy called yesterday! She will be free September the 24th to leave her job, and will join me the following week. I'm so glad she'll be here before Nathan leaves. She said her health is fully restored too.

We also called Tim and Rachel yesterday. It was wonderful to hear voices from home! I wish I could spend a day with them all again. Tim and Rachel are two of my best buddies. That night we prayed that Rachel would have her baby before we go back in the bush, and four hours later Shoshanna called and said that she had just delivered a baby girl named Amy. I was so tickled! Well, I want to send my diary thus far home for everyone to read, so I'd better copy it off soon. I hope it gets across the faithfulness and power of God in answered prayer. This is only the beginning. He hasn't even started yet.

September 21, 1996

"For this man was counted worthy of more glory than Moses, inasmuch as he that hath builded the house hath more honour than the house."
Hebrews 3:3

We are back in Aikram now and staying so busy that I haven't had time to write. The week in Madang was very fruitful and refreshing. We talked to Mom and Dad Saturday and found out that Tim Stoll may be coming to visit in a few weeks. Nathan is really excited about that. I am too. The Williamses were a tremendous help. My crates did not come, but I made arrangements over the phone for them to be brought through customs and put on Lutheran shipping to Madang, where the Williamses will pick them up and put them on MAF to Kenainj. As it was, we had a plane full of cargo—food for four months takes up a lot of room. Pastor Allen and a handful of the older Aikram bunch were at the airstrip to meet us. All the young folks had gone to Simbai for the independence games, and Frank had flown to Lae with his uncle Awong. The road was washed out from all the rain lately, so a truck was out of the question. Pastor Allen arranged for four of the fellowships to come to Kenainj Thursday and carry our stuff. Each fellowship was given ten kina for the church treasury. They got about half the food and all the tin except one piece. The Kenainj folks plan to make another trip on Tuesday next week. Hopefully the road will be fixed by the time the crates are flown up here. Gebi and Steven had put in the posts and floor joist when we arrived, and now (Saturday) all the walls are up and ready for pitpit [pitpit is woven cane]. They plan to have the roof up next week. Nathan has been busy building the most beautiful set of kitchen furniture. Three chairs and one table, and also a desk chair are done. Even Dad would be impressed by the quality Nathan has achieved.

As soon as the gasoline gets up here, he hopes to start cutting the shelving and flooring material. Awong hasn't been by to get his money yet, although I'm sure he will be. The weather is rainy as usual, but the blessing is that we have learned to set out all our containers to be filled and never have to go down to the water source any more to carry water up. We are eating much better this month. Variety makes a world of difference. Language learning is at a slow pace right now. Everyone is gone or busy, me included.

Nathan and I have a vision for all of Papua New Guinea that dominates our conversation and our prayer. So much could be done here. P.N.G. is a free country open to the gospel and the Bible. People are eager, almost desperate, to learn to read and speak English. Correspondence courses in

English would go over with a bang. The Post Offices would let tracts with response cards be placed in every P.O. box, thus reaching all the educated, influential people in the country. There are newspapers, practically given away at every corner, the cheapest way to learn to read Pidgin or English. Every paper is read and studied by dozens of people until it is worn out. Printing tracts or offers of correspondence courses would be cheap and well received. There are hundreds of little villages all around Madang proper that are accessible by automobile and would be open to literature distribution. Most every one under thirty can read some Pidgin, and many can read haltingly in English. All are eager to improve their education since it means better jobs and more money.

Here in the mountain areas, sport holidays would be a key. If, one year in advance, you announced a sport tournament to be held at a certain village, on a certain week, for volleyball, soccer, and basketball, adding that there would be some music, skits, and speakers during the afternoon and evening, as well as a big mumu at the end of the four day party, you could easily expect three to four thousand people of three different main language groups. I intend to try this in a year or so when I know the language a little better and can organize it. I could get Jerry Williams to come as a guest speaker and even Dad could come and do a simple chalk talk each evening with Jerry Williams translating. It would need hours and hours of prayer preparation from a lot of people back home. That is all this country lacks to be blown wide open with revival and salvation: prayer and people. It is on the heart of God and very possible. I can't wait to see it happen.

September 25, 1996
"But God commendeth His love toward us in that while we were yet sinners, Christ died for us." Romans 8:28

I never really appreciated the message of this verse before. How amazing it is that God could and would love us before we loved Him in return. It is so hard, the hardest thing I know, to love unlovable, unappreciative people. And yet, the ministry is loving people, not just by word, but by deed and truth. I've always been sadly short on love for others, and it has hindered ministry toward many people. How can they believe that God loves and accepts them when I obviously don't? "Now abideth these three, faith, hope, and charity, but the greatest of these is charity."

Nathan is gone. He got to studying the radio and solar panel equipment and discovered that we need one hundred feet of wire and some other stuff. Besides, CRMF forgot to include the instructions with the radio and tower. So Nathan walked down to Kenainj this morning to see if he could catch a plane to Madang for a few days and get everything we need. He will probably come back Monday by MAF. It is lonely without him, but it's good for me too, since it is a small preparation for future days. We have been able to play volleyball a few times lately with the ball we brought back from Madang. Language learning is barely progressing at all. I hope when the house is done and the people aren't so busy helping me, we will have more time to spend on language.

The house is ready for the tin now, all the framing done. Nathan has got one month left to build all my shelves and set up the radio and solar panel stuff. Pastor Allen decided that I don't need shelves and that we won't cut any more wood. Nathan told him we were going to have shelves if he had to rip up the floor to make them. He didn't even listen to him. So I went and explained that the home church had sent Nathan out here to make sure I got shelves and a desk and furniture and if he came back to the US without having done what they sent him for, they wouldn't be very happy and neither would I. Oh! And that settled it. I may not have a floor now, but I will have shelves and a desk. Hopefully mister Awong Dingdong will let us cut some more wood and I will have both. We'll see. I think they're getting tired of working for us. I don't know what I would have done if there were no believers here to help and carry. In spite of all the problems and friction, we have been truly blessed. Well, that's all, or as they say in tok ples, Tep and aow.

September 29, 1996

"A new commandment I give unto you, that ye love one another; as I have loved you, that ye also love one another. By this shall all men know that ye are my disciples, if ye have love one to another." John 13:34, 35

Sunday afternoon. I am making it much better all by myself than I thought I would. The people have pulled closer in to take care of me and keep me company since Nathan is gone, and I make more effort to go out among them as well. The volleyball is a big hit, literally. Yesterday while we where playing it started to rain and we all ran for the Kamp Korp and huddled around the fire pits to stay dry.

Jerry and Nataline are two people I like more and more all the time. They are a blessing to me and have taught me without being able to com- municate verbally. I brought my photo album to the Kamp Korp and we had a huddle of about fifteen people all trying to see at once. When the women see the pictures of Mom, they mourn for me loudly crying, "Nant

Ami, ayiiiiayiiiiayiii..soria.." and stroke my arms, assuring me they will take care of me and that my mother need not worry about me. So then I hang my head and mourn with them, just a little louder and they all nod their heads in approval and we go on to the next picture. Culture is fun as long as you know what's going on.

Language learning is rolling again. It's amazing how much extra time I have to study without Nathan around. I've been memorizing dialogues and practical sentences and then going out and using them on whoever is walking by. If they look at me blankly and say, "Mi no savy English." I go study some more. The other day I learned the phrase, "Are you tired?" (Nup mauses gup?) Then I went up toward the Kamp Korup and met Jeshun and Waina just back from the garden, so I tried it out on them. They looked at me astonished, then Jeshun sang out joyfully, "Yaow, Yip mauses gup! Yes, I'm tired!" Then he proceeded to wail loudly his sob story about how hard he worked and how tired he was. It was all acting and everyone was laughing, fit to be tied, so I took my cue and started mourning for him, expressing my pity that he had to work so hard by pretending to cry and patting him and rubbing his bald head in the Kumboi sympathy manner. In an instant the show was over and we were laughing just as hard as everyone else while he retold the whole incident with great expression. By the end of the day everyone had heard and came by to tell me how tired they were. Language learning is a blast!

I also have made leaps and bounds with my guitar. The three lessons that June gave me and the things she taught me about the chord sequences down into the minors and the sevenths have opened doors of music I didn't know existed. I've written three songs and put music to them. My hand is stiff and sore from playing. Thank God for music. Thank God for June!

The Seventh Day Adventists were having a revival this week and there were about 400 people sharing our meager water supply. Every day crowds would come by to see the white lady and stare. If I happened to be outside, they would run up until they were about 20 feet away and stop there in a huddle with as many as 25 others and stare unashamedly until I somehow managed to get out of sight. It was unnerving. I kept the tarps down and the door shut all weekend and stayed in the house as much as possible. They're finally gone, but today the SDA girls from lower Aikram came by to look for a while. It is hard to be friendly when adults stare without shame for unlimited time and strain to look through your windows, but I know ministry depends on me not showing my aggravation. So I smile and shake hands with them one at a time and make a beeline for the house where I hide until I hear them going away. I know I am still too unfriendly for best results, but my sanity couldn't take any more than what I'm giving. Hopefully, in time I will become used to wading through the staring crowds while avoiding stepping on the jaws lying on the ground. Maybe they will grow bored of looking at me too.

Simon, one of the preachers from another fellowship, came by with his wife a little while ago and brought a gift of papaya, bananas and oranges. It was most welcome, to say the least. Oh, and before I forget; Awong came by for his money and signed the receipt I had written up. He said I could cut as much lumber as I need for the house and anything built inside of it as long as I didn't start building any other buildings with it. I asked him if he always keeps his word and if I could trust him. He assured me I could and said he had a receipt for me to sign as well, proving that he had cut all the lumber I needed for the five hundred kina agreed upon. Well, that was A O.K. with me, and he said we could finish cutting a week from now when he returns from Lae. So I guess Nathan will be working on the solar panels and radio all this week, and next week we will finish the sawmill cutting and have two weeks left to get everything built. Gebi and Steven got the tin on the house and the floor down in the storeroom. It is up to the old folks to get the pitpit woven for the walls. Well, my power is beeping, so I'd better close.

October 5, 1996
"Let us therefore fear, lest a promise being left us of entering into his rest, any of you should seem to come short of it." Hebrews 3:1

Well, it is Saturday afternoon. Nathan didn't come until Wednesday evening. He got stuck in Madang because no one was flying this direction. But he got all the supplies needed for putting up the radio and solar system. The solar system, battery hook ups, and lights are all finished, and today he hiked back down to Kenanj for the rope to put up the radio antenna. The folks at Aikram have had rest for two weeks now.

Pastor Allen has gone to Fokefoke for a holiday. The roof is on the house and they have decided to quit for a while. Hopefully, Monday things will start rolling again. Nathan also got the shelves in the storage room built, which was an all day project. I'm so glad he came. None of this would have gotten done if he hadn't.

In town he got news from home. It seems that last week Becky Friedlein died of a heart attack. I was shocked speechless when he told me. Sweet little Becky, barely in her thirties. God spared her life until she could come to know him and gave her less than a year of living below before he took her home. Everyone that knew her will grieve for their loss of a sweet friend and sister, but death truly has no sting when I stop to remember that very soon we shall see her again in Glory.

Nathan also had news from Cathy. Her job is still delaying her, and she doesn't know when she will be able to join me. Hopefully before Nathan leaves. Also, Tim is not coming until later sometime. I can make it here all by myself, but one other person of my same language and culture, whether we have anything in common or not, is a great blessing. To say the very least, once I learn the language and know what is going on a little more, it should be easier. The best place around to learn language and culture is in the Kamp Korp (kitchen house). It is a big, open hut with three fire pits in a row, the length of the building, and two mumu holes in the corner. In the evening, everyone from the youngest to the oldest is squatted in there around the fires talking, eating and recounting the day's events.

Yesterday, some folks from Kongoro brought some meat from a pig they butchered that morning. The Kamp Korp was full of heaps of mbep, sakup, manty, and bauwunt. (greens, pitpit, potatoes, and cassava or tapioca) Every female in the village was in there preparing the mumu while talking and laughing with each other. The stones were piled high on the fires, heating up, and they looked like altars of old, ready for the sacrifice. When everything was ready, the rocks were carefully moved to the mumu pits with a kampus (tongs) and the food placed in the cooking bilams or wrapped in banana leaves on top of the hot stones. This was all covered with another layer of banana leaves, and the rest of the hot stones were piled on top. Hollow bamboo shoots were left sticking out of the mumu and occasionally water was poured down them to help steam the food and keep it tender. While the mumu was cooking, we all played volleyball until Tombi called us in to eat. The mumu was dug up, and everything inside had cooked tender, and was very hot. The pork had been laid in big slabs on top of everything else and had flavored the whole meal. I saw Carolyn running past with a square piece of pig hide with the wiry black hair sticking out about three inches. There was a thick layer of white fat on the under side and grease was dripping off her hands and chin. Three other kids were chasing her, trying to get their share of the treat. Soon everyone had his own piece of pig fat. They would grab a fist full of black bristle to hold it firmly and take huge bites out of the snow white fat. The look on my face as I watched one fellow consume about a cup of lard in two minutes must have caught his attention, because he started laughing and waved the bristle in my direction. "Mi kaikai na kamap strongpela tru." So pig fat makes you strong does it? I think I'll stay a weak white meri [a weak white girl].

The kawkaw was very good however, and the lean meat that had cooked dry on top of everything was quite edible. It is easier than I would have imagined to squat in the smoke in a Kamp Korup filled with happy, chattering natives, munching down on mumu while holding your food out of reach of the chickens, ducks, dogs, and pigletts rushing helter skelter around you in competition for the scraps dropped. How quickly a person can adjust!

Every morning, Fera comes by the house, taking her piglets out to the garden to eat all day. She makes a grunting noise in the back of her throat that sounds just like a mama sow, and the piglets fall in line behind her as they all go grunting toward the garden. It is quite humorous, and I struggle to keep a straight face as she bids me good morning in between snorts. I know I need to write all these little details down before they become so commonplace that I cease to notice them. Nathan will be returning soon, and I really need to get up and start a meal, he should be ravenous after walking over twenty miles with a heavy load.

My computer keeps acting up. The top half of the screen disappears in streaks of color on and off. Maybe it's from the ants that built a nest under the keyboard while we were in Madang. I hope it doesn't completely give out on me. Until later.

[The Jungles of New Guinea just claimed another notebook computer]

October 23, 1996 [Hand written entry]
"I will never leave thee nor forsake thee." Hebrews 13:5
Nathan is gone, and he took my computer with him. It must have gotten a bad case of culture shock, because it passed out completely about two weeks ago. Nathan left Sunday, and this is Thursday. I hate being here alone. Loneliness is a terrible thing, even if you are somewhat used to it. God is being sufficient though, and there are some side benefits. I can now spend 6-7 hours each day in organized language study. I am making definite progress. Also, I seek out the company of the village folks more, squatting by the fire in the Kamp Korup every evening, straining to catch bits and pieces of the conversation flowing around me in the darkness. Rosinda is a blessing, and the radio is a help too. Even if I have nothing to say, it's nice to be able to hear other people speaking English to each other. Only, the radio is on the blink now as well. No wonder these folks are still living in the dark ages; nothing runs or works long in this country. Nathan took a

helicopter out from Kenainj. What a thrill it must be to be on your way home with three months of wild stories to tell. I'm so glad Nathan was able to come with me these first three months. I know I can make it here. It's harder than I thought it would be, but God is bigger than I thought He was too. I can feel His hand and His presence daily, and that alone makes it all worth it. I have no long range goals since I don't know yet what God is planning to do here. And that is hard for me since I have always planned everything and thought every detail out way ahead of time. So right now all I can do is throw myself into language learning and pray for more guidance. I wish I loved this place and these people like I do home and the folks at Cane Creek. I feel guilty for not loving and appreciating this place and these people; maybe that will come later. I hope so. I don't want them to feel like I'm unhappy here with them or that I am dissatisfied, but is there ever any place like Home? Maybe in time this will become home to me. Or maybe the Lord will take us to our real HOME soon. I sure hope so. He can come as soon as yesterday as far as I'm concerned.

Priscilla [Pastor Allen's wife] is the same. Pastor Allen didn't want her to go to town when Nathan did. I guess she'll probably die unless God intervenes. I don't know what is best. I offered to pay her fare out whenever she can go.

Well, my hand is tired. I'm really not as pessimistic as this entry sounds. I am happy, healthy and sane.

October 26, 1996

"God kunup simpnungi, nyinuk nogum Jisas, nip kunup nak, binump ankai ankai di muntmangi namp aiyang ayinpai, kiyuk makunmunpai, ferne ferne mundinpai." John 3:16

How lovely is this verse! Last evening at the kamp korup (community cook house) Natoline hugged me and said; "Nant mapenamp yant aiyang mundipan." I love you with all my liver. I got the translation from Rosinda, and today, during our language lesson, I discovered three different ways to say, "I love you."

Simbur - is all the intestines, and denotes compassion, pity, and sorrow.

Mapun - is the liver, and denotes extreme feeling of affection and emotion.

Muntmangi - is the heart, and although I'm not positive yet, I think it is a little more objective than the liver love, involving choice. A love based on your knowledge of the object's worthiness of that love. It includes respect, trust, belief, and honor.

Therefore we changed John 3:16 and put the compassion love from God toward us and the heart love from us toward God. The literal translation being that we must love Christ with all our heart (trust, knowledge, belief, acceptance) to receive eternal life. It has deep meaning to the Kumboi people. One thing God made sure of at Babel was to put a word or phrase in every language that would communicate His love to the world. I've been thrilled about it all day. I put music to the Kumboi translation and walked up to the kamp korup with my guitar and sang it for them over and over until they were soon singing along with wide grins on their faces. Ferne ferne mundinpai is the favorite line. Forever and ever they will live. Thank you God.

October 30, 1996
"Seeing then that we have an great high priest, that is passed into the heavens, Jesus the son of God, let us hold fast our profession." Hebrews 4:14

There is so much I should be writing down and no time to write it all. I shall go as far as I am able. There are scores of people here in the village. Jashun's old, blind sister, that I had pictures of in my slides, died two days ago, and relatives came from everywhere. She said she was going to heaven, but she was also senile, so I don't know if she had been saved or not. They buried her on the mountain in a plain wooden coffin and said a few words over her grave, then they came back and feasted, and they're still at it two days later. This is pig-killing season, and they plan to mumu and slaughter ten big hogs tomorrow. Today they are mumuing the taro. Half of the relatives that came for the burial have stayed behind for the mumu.

I am not getting my afternoon study time since I go up to the Kamp Korup and sit in the smoke with everyone and visit. That is intense language and culture study since everyone talks to me continually and makes me properly repeat them and respond. Squeals of delight ring out when I say something unprompted that makes sense. Teaching me their language is a favorite game, and even the unsaved from other villages come to have a try at it. I hope it lasts, because I'm learning quickly this way. I'm beginning to enjoy their company too, and seek them out instead of avoiding them. It no longer bothers me as bad as it did to have someone grab my head, bend it side ways and claw through my hair to see if I have lice, all the while exclaiming loudly to everyone how clean my hair and scalp are. Last night I finished my reading and memorization by 7:30 and could not sleep, so I wandered up toward the Kamp Korup and met Alice and Yaras heading toward Ben and Sonya's house with a flaming pandanus torch. They took me by the hand and led me home with them. Ben and Sonya, Rosinda, and two other visitors were seated around the morup (fire place) and made room for us. "Daughter," says Ben, "I'll be very happy when you learn our language and I can come tell you stories about the old days." Rosinda told them I knew John 3:16 in tokples, and there was a chorus of "angan!" (say it), so I did. Alice cried and laughed and beat me with the palms of her hands all at the same time. They were all making quite a din. It was an encouraging response, to say the least.

I discovered that Allen lied to me last year when he said he was the leader of 7,000 people in twenty villages that all spoke the same dialect. In truth, there are three villages, totaling less than 300 people that speak this dialect. The other dialects are similar in syntax and morphology and can be understood by the "Yimbe Munum" Kumboi speakers. But they're all very different when written.

I don't know what God's will is here, but I know I'm in it. My path has been one of walking through doors that God has opened, so I know I am in the center of His will. And it is clearly evident that He is answering prayer in language learning. What can He have planned for these people? I wish I knew, but until them I can only pray and obey. And keep on believing that He is able and not willing that any should perish.

November 1, 1996
"Therefore leaving the principles of the doctrine of Christ, let us go on unto perfection; Not laying again the foundation of repentance from dead works and faith toward God." Hebrews 6:1

I'm halfway through the 6th chapter of Hebrews now and can say it straight through from chapter one. It seems to help me remember language better, keeping my memory exercised with scripture. This is language study time right now, being 9:00 A.M., Friday morning, but the details of yesterday's mumu are still fresh in my mind, so I decided to write them down. A lot of new folks came that I've never met, all related somehow, some saved and some not.

Yesterday morning eight pigs were led up toward the kamp korup and tied to stakes set in the ground a distance apart. Jerry killed the first two, his and Bill's, by hitting them over the head with a club. The first blow counts the most because if you don't blind the pig and hopefully knock the sense out of it, it gets mad and will fight for it's life. They all seem to loathe killing their pigs, going about it with a grim determination. The throat is then cut and the head saved for later. The intestines are removed and the carcass cut in four pieces: belly, back, and sides with front and back leg attached. The women take the intestines and wash them out and cut them into about two-foot lengths, tying one end shut. Then they proceed to stuff them full of all the other odds and ends, tendons, bits of meat, guts, and organs. The children dart around here and there, sneaking bits of meat or intestines to lay on the rocks that are heating on huge fires for the mumu. Then they wait, hopping back and forth with great anticipation, occasionally sprinting forward into the intense heat of the fire to flip their treat over and scorch the other side. When the outside is sufficiently black to hide the raw inside, they pop it into their mouths, blowing around it noisily to keep from burning their tongue as they race back to the piles of raw meat for another piece to roast. Large sheets of tree bark are bent in a circle about six feet in diameter and 2 ½ feet deep and staked in position. The bottom of this tremendous cooking pot is lined with banana leaves, and the first layer of red-hot rocks on top of that. Now the food: meat, potatoes, cassava, shredded green banana, taro, pumpkin, yam, rock melon, and greens are carefully placed, wrapped in leaves with hot rocks scattered evenly throughout, and more on top until the bark container is full. When completely finished, it looks like a pile of steaming rocks and banana leaves. It is left to simmer two or three hours. The meat, hair still attached, is not completely cooked, only semi-preserved for later smaller mumu's during the rest of the week. Relatives and invited visitors carry pre-determined pieces back to their own villages, later repaying with the exact same cut of meat from their own local pigs and mumu. They worked until late last night, and right before bedtime, made their last mumu's with the pig heads, choice greens, and taro. These were left to cook overnight and dug up the next morning for a breakfast feast. Everything but the hair is eaten. I saw teenage girls digging the eyeballs out of a pig head and sucking on them, and little kids running around with a juicy snout half chewed.

Mama Fera came running up with a light green tree frog she had caught, about three inches long, and tossed him on the hot mumu rocks to scorch like the children do their treats. "When I was young, at my village, I used to love to eat frogs," she explained to me with a giggle before crunching down. Every now and then someone would dart a look at my face to see if I was disgusted or horrified. I documented the whole day with a roll of film and celebrated by barbecuing six ribs over my own fire. It was quite a day, and I must say, mumu's are a lot of fun!

November 5, 1996

"Wherein God, willing more abundantly to show unto the heirs of promise, the immutability of his counsel, confirmed it by an oath: That by two immutable things, in which it was impossible for God to lie, we might have a strong consolation, who have fled for a refuge to lay hold upon the hope set before us." Hebrews 6:17-18

I, who have always been a stickler for routine and consistency, am having a time keeping awake and interested in language studies. It should be easier when I get my crates and can start using the tapes and 3x5 cards. Bro. Jerry Williams came up on the radio today and said that my crates are through customs and should arrive in Madang today. Praise the LORD!! Also, he is sending my mail and the things Nathan bought up by Island Airways tomorrow morning. I plan to walk down with Rosinda and Jerry and Natoline tomorrow to get it. I hope I'm fit enough to take a ten hour hike on bad trails. They started work on my house yesterday, gathering pitpit and making shutters. We are short of lumber—three windows and one door, plus some flooring, beds, and shelves. I pray that Awong will keep his bargain and finish cutting the last log. I also talked to Cathy on the radio a couple of days ago. She plans to join me in December. The house should be livable by then and I'll certainly be glad for her company. I feel a spiritual heaviness today that weighs me down, I guess I need to pray.

November 6, 1996

"Which hope we have as an anchor of the soul, both sure and stedfast, which entereth into that within the veil. Whither the forerunner is for us entered, even Jesus, made an high priest forever after the order of Melchisedec." Hebrews 6:19-20

How altogether lovely is the word of God! How could I ever translate it without the constant guidance of the Holy Spirit and hours of prayer!

Well, I walked to Kenainj and back today. I left at 6:00 A.M. and returned at 3:30 P.M. That makes 9 ½ hours of walking and climbing. I feel like one of those pavement roller things went over my lower torso, but I made it. And I got my mail! Most of it was a couple months old, but it was better to me than manna from Heaven! I got letters from home folks and people I've never met before. It was so encouraging to read about the love and prayers of so many people for ME. Proverbs 25:25 says, *"As cold waters to a thirsty soul, so is good news from a far country."* I think I could safely say that that is an understatement. God is so good in having given me so many friends; so many love and pray for me.

Time is passing quickly now. I've been in P.N.G. for four months already. The loneliness is getting easier to bear. Loneliness isn't really being alone; it's not being able to communicate in your own heart language and culture and be perfectly understood. It's not being able to talk about deep, important things with someone who's background and world-view is much the same as your own. How lonely Jesus must have been as He walked this earth! There was no one who had anything in common with Him, no one He could talk about the old days with. No one that knew Him and understood the things He said. "In all things it behooved him to be made like unto his brethren that he might be a merciful and faithful high priest."

The rain is pouring out of the sky as though it were poured from a bucket. I am so tired I shall skip memorization tonight and start chapter seven tomorrow. I wish I could leave my body and float up far enough away to view this work of God in Aikram objectively. What is He doing here? What am I doing here? What lies ahead? What should be aimed for, prayed for, and accomplished? Tell me, God, what are our goals?

Yes, I want to walk by sight and not by faith. I want to read the last chapter and make sure the end of the story is everything I hope it will be. God??????? I'm beginning to understand all those Psalms that begin with *"Wait upon the LORD."* Patience is a virtue and tribulation worketh patience, so I guess I'd better shut up before I get blessed with enough tribulation to teach me patience. I'm so tired, I'm rambling like our old farm truck. Don't let me mess this up, God. There are so many people—children—following my footsteps, watching me, admiring me. If they only knew! God, help me be exactly what I should be for the sake of the reinforcements coming behind me.

LOVE

The first and greatest commandment is to love the Lord your God with all your heart, soul, mind and strength and your neighbor as yourself. Why was that last phrase added? Because you cannot love God without loving your neighbor.

Love is a river without banks that cannot flow in any one, narrow channel. It does not choose who may drink from its waters and who may not, but flows freely to all without respect of persons. The waters of Love increase every time they touch and minister to someone in their path until, by the time the river reaches the ocean, love is a mighty wall of water that cannot be stayed.

And so also, as one goes about each day loving in word and deed, every person one comes in contact with, at the end of the day, when we bow our head and say, "I love you, Lord," the statement will hold all the weight of a mighty wall of water, and God will turn and look at us with surprise and deep appreciation and say, "Why, so you do!"

For that is the sort of Love He gave, and that is the Love He's looking for.

November 11, 1996
"O LORD, thou art my God; I will exalt thee, I will praise thy name; for thou hast done wonderful things; thy counsels of old are faithfulness and truth. Isaiah 25:1

This is Sunday, and everyone is at the volleyball court. Priscilla is here playing the guitar. She looks remarkably better since she's been taking the medicine I gave her.

Leah, the deaf girl I named last year, has been here the last two days. I think she has finally caught on that there must be a way of communication with the hands. When ever I see her, I sign her name—an L down the jaw—and then my name—an R down the jaw, but she usually just giggles and looks away like she thinks I'm making fun of her. But today, after service, I started signing whole sentences to her and pointing to various objects and signing their name. The other girls would all copy me and no one was laughing. I could see it suddenly dawn on her that I was talking with my hands, for she got very intent and started copying me, much more accurately than the others and pointing to different objects, signing the name I had shown and looking at me for affirmation. Could it be that Leah may someday be able to "hear" the gospel? I wish I knew sign language better and had some idea about how to teach her. She is intelligent, I think. She has a pretty face too, but when she smiles you can see most of her teeth are missing. Most of the folks here have terrible teeth. And their breath smells like an open grave. Well, that's all my news for now.

November 20, 1996
"And it is yet far more evident: for that after the similitude of Melchisedec there ariseth another priest. Who is made, not after the law of a carnal commandment, but after the power of an endless life." Hebrews 7:15-16

This really will not do. I must keep up with my diary better than this. What has happened in the last 10 days? First and foremost, my crates came to Madang and Jerry Williams sent them by MAF to Kenainj on Monday. I walked down to receive them with Rosinda. Ten of them came on the big Twin Otter (that plane covers the airstrip) and four got left in Madang—too many kilos. So I stayed the night at Septimas' house and was treated like a queen. I discovered that some years earlier he looked after some other white missionaries, and when they left they gave him a sewing machine and sixty kina. Thanks to their generosity, Septimas and his wife can't do enough for me. The next morning, most of Aikram came down to see Gebi (the carpenter that built my house) off. Island Airways came at 9:00 A.M., and I arranged for them to bring the other crates on Thursday. We met the Haus Sik truck (hospital truck) on its way to Aiome and hired them to come down and pick up all the crates and carry them up to Sakup (bush trail junction) on Thursday as well. Rosinda and I and all the girls headed back to Aikram. I ran all the way down the trail and made it from Fogefoge in an hour and a half. I've named the bush trail between Sakup and Aikram. On the way up, it's "Sheer Misery." On the way down it's "Home Free." I can run down it, but climbing it is as laborious as breathing underwater. Anyway, the crates. I got back in time for the last radio scheduled time and received message that the other four crates are coming today, Wednesday, by MAF. But when I woke up this morning, it was pouring and looks like it may rain all day. So I don't know if the truck or the plane will come. Pastor Allen is insistent that I let them open all the crates at the top of the trail and divide the load up into bilams, I think it's half curiosity to see what's inside, because he also wanted the list of everything. Rosinda said it wouldn't be any problem to carry it down intact. I said "No," but he pretended like he didn't hear me and said I could make the decision later. Sometimes I'd like to haul off and kick him so hard that he'd die of old age before he came down. In this culture a man has four things of value and intelligence: his children, his pigs, his wife and his dog—in that order. Women should be lied to about anything and everything lest they come to think they are important. They should be ignored completely unless screaming hysterically. I just love it and fit in perfectly! The only thing the women have over the men here is strength (they do all the work) and if a husband gets too out-of-line, his wife may beat him up. Is that warped or what? A woman can own nothing of value, so it's perfectly reasonable for Pastor Allen to take everything I've got and kindly let me use it. I've about decided that what I need is a beard, or a husband, both of which are hard to come by out here.

I'm seated in my smokehouse right now, on a pile of logs, occasionally turning two ears of corn on the fire, trying to evenly burn the husk off. It's the best way in the world to eat corn. I made a deal with the girls: if they bring me potatoes and corn, I'll give them rice and tin meat. Keeps us both happy.

Later. It's about 8:30 now, and the sky has started to clear off a little. Jerry and Dick just went by, headed for Sakup with the tarp. I'm inside my new house now. All the interior walls are done except the one between my room and the living room. I wove one all by myself, but Rosinda informed me, with a little awe and embarrassment, that women are not supposed to be able to weave blinds. The sheets of woven pitpit are just barely stuck to the wall with a block of wood here and there - we need 1x2's and 1x3's to nail it up properly and are waiting on Awong to cut the rest of the timber. I went down to talk to him three times, and he was always gone. Finally I managed to catch him and give him the tape measure that Nathan had sent and request that he finish cutting the timber I need for the floor, windows, and blinds. He said something about "next year," and I must have got my "you're mud" look on my face because he changed his mind and said three weeks. I'm going to remind him again next week, and I told him I would. He just laughed. He's an ornery old fellow, but at least he's an honest ornery, and I appreciate that.

Jerry and Natoline are two of my favorites here. Natoline is about my age and expecting her fourth baby. She is about as primitive as they come, but entirely without guile. I learn a lot about this culture from just being around her, because she doesn't hesitate to correct me when I'm out of line and does not make any effort to hide their ways or customs, lest I be shocked or offended. Once I came into the Kamp Korup to ask Steven a question—and remained standing to do so since I had no intention of staying. Natoline gave a clucking noise of disapproval and said in tok ples, "Sit down first, then talk! It is rude to speak while standing up." Another time I picked up her toddler, Lazarus, who never wears a diaper, and she warned me in Pidgin, "Ass bilong em i doti." (He's got a dirty ass.) Now most of the folks here know that word brings a funny response from Europeans, but they're not sure why. In Pidgin, the word 'ass' means bottom, base, beginning, first, original—no evil connotations, and no butts about it. I nearly fell off my log/pew the first time I heard them preach Jesus Christ the same Ass-day, today, and forever. You see, yesterday is today's ass, right? And when they ask what hometown you're from, they ask where your ass place is. I don't think I'll ever get used to that one, it makes me cringe. The joys of language learning!

Well, it's now the end of the day, and it has started raining again, so the truck driver passed the word by radio that he would come down tomorrow. I spent the day bleaching the doors, windows, walls of the storage room, and my room to get rid of the mildew.

November 22, 1996

"For the law made nothing perfect, but the bringing in of a better hope did; by the which we draw nigh to God." Hebrews 7:19

Well, yesterday dawned bright and sunny, and everybody went up to Sakup to wait for the truck that never came. They are tired of that now, and only Pastor Allen went today. I don't know what happened to the truck. Yesterday, at the radio's morning scheduled time, Nathan called. I didn't recognize his voice. They wanted to make sure I was alright after being in the bush all by myself for a month. They also said that Tim and Gabe want to come in January/February of 1997. They bought me a 4-wheeler and are working on getting it shipped with the Lindseys' cargo in December. Boy will it be nice to not have to make a 10 hour hike to get mail or tote groceries! Pastor Allen has already offered to drive it for me! He says he'll take over the chain saw for me too.

Steven is faithfully working on the interior walls now. He's the slowest human being I ever met, but lucky for me, he's a perfectionist and doesn't quit until the job is finished.

Mom said for me to ask for one of Pastor Allen's puppies, so yesterday I took some leftover goose bones and skin from my lunch to look at them and see if they are big enough to eat food yet. I crushed the bones up into a slimy goo and they sucked it off my fingers. A crowd of kids gathered around me, squealing in delight when the puppies started growling at each other over their first taste of real food. One of the kids started yelling, "Me, me, me!" Naturally, I assumed she wanted to feed the puppies too, so I scooped a lump of goo out with the same two fingers the puppies had been licking and dumped it in her grimy palm. She immediately stuffed it in her mouth and the other kids all howled in jealousy. The puppies did too, and I wasn't sure which party I was feeding any more. Anyway, I chose a fat spotted one (puppy) and named it MinMin, which is Kumboi for joy or happiness. It will be fun to have some company, even if it is only a mutt. They're still too little to leave their mother now.

Well, language learning is not going as fast as I hoped it would. I have to remind myself that I'm learning two languages at once and have no helps—like my books and paper and computer. Gabe and Tim will probably bring me a new computer and the crates will have my books and papers. I try to study, but my mind drifts like an unanchored boat, and I can't seem to remember anything. The only time I remember a word is when I make a mistake and get corrected. Like in Pidgin, the other day the girls asked me what American women wore, as far as clothing. I replied matter of factly that most of them wore pants. They all giggled in embarrassment and assured me that they did too, to which I must have looked surprised because they asked curiously if I did or not. I said "Well, no." About that time I noticed that Rosinda, my language helper, was about to explode with silent laughter. I demanded to know what was so funny, and she explained that in Pidgin, pants mean underwear, and that pants, as in jeans or slacks, are called trousers.

Oops. That brings to mind an incident a few days earlier. One of the preacher boys here, a very dignified older fellow, has a bright blue pair of trousers, and I noticed a stranger in the village walking around with them on. So sometime during the day I turned to the preacher man standing nearby and asked innocently, "Aren't those your pants?" For a moment he looked positively terrified, no doubt wondering when and where I had seen his underwear and if he had been wearing them at the time. Then he followed the direction of my gaze and recognized his bright blue trousers and sighed a relieved agreement. Somehow language lessons like that stick in your mind.

Also songs remain in my memory. I translated Happy all the Time into Pidgin and tok ples (Kumboi), and they all loved it, me included. In doing so, I discovered the word for sin, which is gach, meaning stained, spotted, filthy. I also discovered the word for cleanse, which is wikak, a verb meaning to rub out or erase, to wipe clean. So I guess language learning isn't going so terribly slow after all, I just expect more than I should. Well, it is radio time, so I have got to go now.

November 25, 1996

"And Hezekiah received the letter from the hand of the messengers, and read it: and Hezekiah went up unto the house of the LORD, and spread it before the LORD. And Hezekiah prayed unto the LORD saying, O LORD of Hosts, God of Israel, that dwellest between the cherubim, thou art the God, even thou alone, of all the kingdoms of the earth, thou hast made Heaven and earth. Incline thine ear, O LORD, and hear; open thine eyes and see: and hear all the words of Sennacherib, which hath sent to reproach the living God." Isaiah 37:14-17

I found this story yesterday while reading Isaiah and continued to study the life and reactions of Hezekiah in II Kings as well. I saw that whenever trouble struck, Hezekiah immediately *"spread it before the LORD."* He wasn't brave like Joshua nor full of faith like Moses, but his prayer life time and again protected him from eminent evil. What an encouragement! May I grasp this key to victory.

The truck never came, and we don't know what held it up. This is
Monday again, and whether or not anyone is going up to Sakup to wait on
the truck, I don't know.

Priscilla is feeling fine now and still taking the medicine I gave her. We
practiced a song, The Lighthouse, and sang it as a special yesterday. She has
a pretty tenor that blends well with my low lead.

I felt sort of sick yesterday afternoon and went to bed at 6:30, waking
up at 5:30 this morning. I went out and sat on the Ponder Rock to watch
the sunrise. The Ponder Rock sits out beside my new house and overlooks
the mountains and valleys and lowlands all the way out to the ocean. Many
people stop and sit there and ponder the view, so I call it the Ponder Rock.
The mountains get bluer and hazier the farther away they are, until eventually the horizon is lost as the sky and earth meet in a vague blue mist of
clouds. It gives one the feeling of being in a very large corner, at the end
of the earth, as if there were nothing and no one beyond you. As I sat there
waiting on the sun, I remembered a conversation I had on the radio a few
days ago with a missionary, somewhere in the Goroka area. There was no
one else on the frequency so we introduced ourselves and talked a while.
He and his wife are Australian, but he was raised in P.N.G. as an M.K.
(missionary kid). He heard that I was learning the tok ples (local tribal
language), with the intention of translation, and asked if he might give me
his opinion and advice. Of course I said yes, so he proceeded to tell me
of missionary after missionary that had spent twenty plus years in P.N.G.
learning tok ples and translating, only to have the people ignore it for the
Pidgin trade language or go away to learn English. He said all this without
condescension or criticism, stating that he was concerned about the huge
waste of missionary effort when there was so much need in other areas. He
gave allowance that it might be profitable for the Kumboi since I'm so far
into the interior and few people can read Pidgin or English, but pointed
out that the whole country is moving rapidly away from tok ples and toward English and Pidgin. Everything he said was true and spoken from an
unbiased, intelligent point of view, and it shook me up more than a little.
Fortunately, like Hezekiah, I went straight from the radio to my knees and
begged God for an answer. I reminded Him of all the people praying for
me and of all the children and young people that are watching me from a
distance, who might someday follow in my example. I reminded Him of
all the preparation He has put me through and the vision He had given me
from the start. I reminded him of my obedience to go through every open
door He has set before me and of His promise to direct my paths as long as

I trust Him. I reminded Him of all the hours I've spent in prayer, seeking His perfect will and desiring it with a sincere heart. And when at last I finished reminding Him of all these things, I realized that my confidence had been restored and, in truth, He had been reminding me. Then I sat in silence and He began to speak. "I sent you here with a vision for translation, yes. But if that were taken away, would there be nothing left to do? How many times have you wished and prayed for more laborers to take up other areas of ministry?" Then He began to open my eyes to one need after another, each greater than the last. The women and children here are ignored. No women's meetings or Sunday school for the children. Both run wild during the services and cause disturbance. The need for literacy work is enormous. A reading class two or three times a week for Pidgin and English would be very profitable and a way to reach the unbelievers in the other villages that want to learn how to read. The very greatest need He showed me was for a Bible school to train the multitude of preacher boys in these mountains that don't have the money to go to town and pay tuition. There are more being saved each week, and the way to reach a national is with a national. This is a need I cannot meet, as it would require a man to do the teaching, or several, but I can pray for it, and will. And then there are all the little needs like medical work, teaching on cleanliness and childcare. "Do what you can," God said, "There is more than enough work." Then I realized that He hadn't taken away my vision, but increased it tenfold. I am still persuaded that a New Testament in tok ples and Pidgin both would be a great help to these people. But the other needs should not be ignored in my quest to learn tok ples. I was overwhelmed at the stability of God once again. There is no guessing, hide and seek, catch-the-will-of-God-if-you-can. He is sure and steadfast, a shelter in the time of storm, the Rock that is Higher than I. Dependable and faithful. As Hezekiah said, *"thou art the God, even thou alone."*

November 28, 1996

"In everything give thanks for this is the will of God in Christ Jesus concerning you." I Thessalonians 5:18

Yesterday, Rosinda and I went up to the Sakup junction to wait in case the truck came by. We had four hours to talk (the truck went to Aiome). I took the opportunity to describe in detail Thanksgiving day at home. She had never heard of the holiday. I imagined our big old farm table heavy laden with Nanny's good cooking and told about the turkey and dressing and all the pies and cakes. I described the family and all the many things we have to be thankful for, concluding that it was my very favorite holiday. She asked with concern what I was going to do this year for Thanksgiving, since none of the food I described grows on the kawkaw vines here. I replied with a rueful grin that I was going to eat tin fish and rice and be thankful for all the wonderful Thanksgivings I've had. I said that I'd think of Nathan as I eat and laughed because I know that he'll think of me as he gorges himself on cheesecake and pecan pie and enjoy it even more.

This morning when I stumbled out into the mist to build my breakfast fire, Papa Ben already had the fire made and was chopping more wood. "My daughter," says he, "you did not eat since yesterday morning, you must be very hungry." I agreed that I was, and tossed two ears of corn on coals to roast. Then I heard a sound behind me and turned to see Rosinda standing there with a prize chicken in her arms. "Here is your Thanksgiving turkey," she said. My eyes blurred so that I couldn't see straight, and I dove at her, hugging her so hard that both she and the chicken squawked in protest. "It's Ben's chicken," she explained. He added, "I know that if I give this blessing away, God will give me another." I hope and pray that God gives him so many chickens he won't know what to do with them all. I fried my chicken for lunch and enjoyed every bite. So all of you that felt sorry for me on Thanksgiving Day can just put your sorry up, because I had one of the best.

That evening, upon my invitation, the whole village gathered under the florescent light in my new house to hear "The Thanksgiving Story." I took my small globe and started with the world itself, pointing out continents and oceans and important countries. Then I took them to Israel and began with creation, moving swiftly through history as I explained how the human race spread up into Europe. I described England's persecution of Christians and the quest for a new, free country. I added all the details of sickness, hunger, prayer and hope on the Mayflower and finally the discovery of land. I explained that they had no food and were dying until the natives (Indians) came out of the bush and shared their food. Then I described the first Thanksgiving meal and concluded that many of the Indians got saved when they heard about Jesus. There was not a bored expression in the room, and many a sigh of satisfaction as the story ended. Then came about ten minutes of comments like, "So that's what the world looks like," and "So that's what has been happening since Christ died," "There's so much water!" "Papua New Guinea is so tiny; how did the white girl ever find us?" And I realized that I had filled many a gap and answered many a question with one simple story. They saw themselves as the Indian benefactors feeding the starving white meri (woman). I asked them if they would like to say what they are thankful for, and during the next hour, every one of them, some many times, gave thanks to God. Lioni was thankful that her mother had not killed her when she was born, even though she had too many children. Jerry was thankful for prayer and Natoline (Jerry's wife) was thankful for Jerry, which made him giggle in embarrassment and everybody laughed. Ben was thankful for my solar light and batteries. Every one of them mentioned their thanks to Nyinuk nogum Jisas, God's only begotten Son, and thanked God for saving Allen so he could return and bring them the gospel message. When all had said their last thanks, Jerry prayed and we all departed. It was truly one of the best Thanksgivings I can ever remember, and one I shall surely never forget.

December 6, 1996

"Now of the things which we have spoken, this is the sum: We have such an high priest who is set down on the right hand of the throne of the Majesty in the heavens;" Hebrews 8:1

I am seated in my new house. The past week has been a flurry of activity until today. Last Thursday, I went down to talk to Awong (sawmill man) about cutting the rest of the timber for my house. He said two or three more weeks, next year sometime, etc. Then he asked me to pick up five cartons of lamb flaps for him when I go to Madang, ten days from now. I said, "Sure, if my house is finished by then." They started cutting Monday, but he wanted another two hundred kina. I agreed on one hundred and fifty when the job was done. They finished cutting yesterday and used another whole tree. The sawmill gave up the ghost just as they filled my quota of lumber. Pastor Allen, Jerry, Dick, and Lawrence all helped him free of charge. Steven kept building, and the floor is now entirely finished, and there is a gate on the porch. They want to wait for the hand saw in my crates before they do the window shutters. Which brings me to the crates.

There was a tremendous rain two days before the truck was scheduled to come pick up my crates, resulting in numerous landslides between Aiome and Simbai. It won't be passable until a bulldozer reconstructs the road, which may be years. So no truck. Can they carry it all that far by foot? I don't even think about it anymore. They are simply not worth the worry and headache they've been. I believe some of the Aikram folks may open the #2 crate and divide it into bilams (string bags) to carry it all up. It has the tools Steven needs and the paper I need.

It is wonderful to be in my own house. All day yesterday I moved stuff in. People hung around waiting for me to open the storage room so they could see all my food lined up on the shelves. I kept it locked, much to their disappointment. I heard a few irritated comments about it. I trust all the folks here, but it is unwise for the rich man to flaunt his riches before the poor. If they knew how much food and money I have, they would be discontent with what God has given them, and It could even cause them to stumble into covetousness. Everything I give Priscilla has to be given in secret because they get angry with her for not sharing equally everything she gets. The society here is slightly communistic, "what's yours is mine, what's mine is yours" sort of thing.

Priscilla was just here to tell me that Jerry shot a cassowary (emu, ostrich) with his homemade shotgun, and everyone is going to Suluk water where Natoline is preparing it for mumu. They are all pretty excited about it. They love the cassowary meat. I think I'll stay here though, I made that hike yesterday to carry lumber down. Had to scoot on my bottom across one of the landslides. One of these days I'm going to fall right into Heaven.

Less than a week now before I go to town. I may be taking Rosinda with me. I haven't heard from Cathy in ages and am beginning to wonder if she will ever come.

Until later…

December 11, 1996
"For I will be merciful to their unrighteousness, and their sins and their iniquities will I remember no more." Hebrews 8:12

Wednesday morning.

I am sitting in my fine house. Why in the world did God give me a house this nice? I've been pondering that question the last two days. It's not a Better Homes and Gardens feature, but it's better than most missionaries have and a whole lot better than I expected to get. I've got a real wood floor and you can't get anything bigger than a hairpin through the cracks in the boards. I've got window shutters too. If you look close enough you might notice the whittle marks, wedges, and the shims and slivers that went into making them square, but at first glance they're really lovely. And the windows are so big, all seven of them. Something about big windows and high ceiling makes a house seem nicer than it is. The light it allows, probably. The house itself is big enough for a small family and more than adequate for one single girl. The only drawback is that it's the nicest hut most of these folks have ever seen, and there has been a constant flow of sightseers coming to look at the house and me.

A few days ago, Monday, six people went down to Kenainj and opened crate #2 and carried everything up that was in it. So Steven has a good saw now and is finishing the last window shutter today. Rosinda, Luke, and I dug up those two huge stumps out in front of the steps and leveled the ground. Then others took interest and came by and we moved my cook-house over and set it up two strides away from the last front step. I've been piddling on it the last few days. I laid a rock walk that cuts out 50% of the mud I track in.

Well, Rosinda won't be going with me to Madang. She quit coming around for about a week and then left for another village for a week. I can understand the girls' gossip more than they realize, and heard them all talking about Rosinda. Anna is behind it all, I think. They are jealous and accused her of avoiding work and being the white meri's wantok (best friend) and taunted her that maybe she's trying to turn white. Jealousy and the tongue are a bad combination, to say the least. Rosinda was pretty upset and left for another village, staying gone a week. She's back now and has been by to see me. I managed to convey that I knew what was going on and sympathized. But I think it would cause a greater breach between her and her sisters if I took her with me now. In any case, Priscilla offered to go with me, and she really does need a break too. She has been sick for so long and is originally from the coast too, so she would love to get out for a week. Which might be better for me anyway since she'd be closed mouthed about how much money I spend and what I buy. I'm looking forward to the week out and talking to my folks again.

Language learning is going again. I got some paper and other needed items in crate #2. Rosinda and I are slowly working our way through the Kalam dictionary that Lyle Shultz made, adding, deleting, and changing words to fit this dialect as we go. We are in the middle of B now. This will enable me to have the language down in writing before I can even under-stand or speak it fluently and give me more material to study, cutting down on the time spent hunting for vocabulary and culture too. Rosinda is smart and learning English faster than I am learning tok ples. Time to cook lunch.

December 14, 1996

"Looking for that blessed hope, and the glorious appearing of the great God and our Savior Jesus Christ;"Titus 2:13

At the sunrise every morning
As the darkness slips away
I search the clouds with longing
Will my Lord return today?
In the noonday I am listening
For his knock upon the door
At each sound my heart is pounding
Could it be this is my Lord?
In the fading of the sunset
In the cool of every eve
I wait beside my window
Lest my Lord should beckon me.
In the midnight I am wakeful
For the radiance of the moon
Makes me think that he is coming
And his glory floods the room.
Ah! Rejoice my soul - He cometh!
Our Beloved is on his way
Be ever watchful, praying
He may return today.

The other day I read back over this diary and was dumbfounded. I had no idea I had changed so much. Is it the prayer every day? The memorization? Is it the service or being so alone? Is it all of that? Why didn't God change me this rapidly at home? Maybe it's the tribulation. Tribulation worketh patience, and patience hope, and hope maketh not ashamed. I was ashamed reading the first part of this diary. It made me wonder what glaring faults do I have now that I am blind to? With all my heart I want to be perfect in all my ways. I crave to be righteous, to understand the mind of God. To feel the love and compassion He feels for those that are "ignorant and out of the way." I want to get a full view of His glory and holiness. To see through His eyes in every circumstance. I want Eternity Future, I guess. Maybe it is this intense desire to know God like a man knows his friend that had allowed God to change me. But where did that desire come from? God. To God be the glory.

This is Saturday afternoon. Priscilla and I will be walking to Kenainj to-morrow after service. A bunch of folks will come down with us and open two or three more crates and carry it back up. Kenainj is a pretty wild place lately. Last week there was a rape - this week a hold-up. I pray God protects my cargo at Septimas' store.

I changed my language learning technique for this coming year. It is not difficult at all, but if I stick with it, I should know around 2,000 words and a couple hundred dialogues and texts by January. '98, which is a language learned. Also Pidgin should come quickly. I shall continue memorizing two Bible verses a day and, after finishing Hebrews, go on to the book of Jonah, then Ruth. Stories will be fun to quote. I've never had the opportunity to memorize like this before. Well, that is all the news for now. But I think I shall record here a poem I wrote back in March, before I came to P.N.G., and the sequel, which I wrote two days ago.

Sunshine or Shadows
3/28/1996

Hand in hand I've walked beside Him
In the sunshine of my days
And with joy I've always followed
Down the flower strewn pathways.
He has led me with His blessings
Far from all my toil and care
O'er the mountain tops we've wandered
Great the sweetness we have shared
But He pauses in the sunlight
See Him pointing at the shade
Will I follow Him in darkness,
In the hard times still obey?
He is leading off the mountain
To the valleys down below
Thorns and thistles in the pathway
He is saying, "Will you go?"
"Will you follow through the shadows
Gladly go where'r I lead,
Finding souls that dwell in darkness
So that they may walk with me?"
And I, looking in His eyes now,

Rejoice to see the promise bright
He will never never leave me
In the darkest hour of night.
While we travel through the valley
He's a loyal, faithful friend.
Surely, someday we'll go walking
In the sunlight once again.

Sunshine in Shadows
12/12/1996

There's a sunshine in the valley
Sweeter than the mountain's light
And His beams are ever dearer
With the advent of the night
There are trials in the valley
But I'm walking with a friend
And I know that He'll be with me
To the great and glorious end
There are blessings in the valley
Greater than the lofty heights
Precious treasures in the darkness
Waiting for the gift of life
There's a oneness with the Savior
In the valley down below
Had I lingered on the mountain
I would never have come to know
There are shadows in the pathway
Dark - the shadows of the grave
And the dead are all about me
Chained in sin's evil decay
Ah! But death has been defeated
And there's victory o'er the night
So I shall fear no evil
For I'm walking with the Light!

December 25, 1996

"And whatsoever ye shall ask in my name, that will I do, that the Father may be glorified in the Son." John 14:13

Still no computer to keep diary. Dad is sending me his laptop though, with all the newest programs. Last week Priscilla and I went to Madang for supplies. It was miserably hot. We went to the ocean on Saturday to swim, and the water was hot too. I went by Island Air both ways and had 400 kgs of cargo. They gave me a discount on the cargo. We had the entire plane, an islander. In preparation for our trip back on Monday, we couldn't find a ride to the hangar to carry all our stuff. Then on Sunday, another mission-ary family took the flat next to ours, and after meeting them, they offered to take us out to the hangar the next morning. They are the Dennis Wells family, in southern highlands, with Word for the World Baptists Missions. A very nice family. I fear I talked too much; it had been so long since I had an American to talk to, I must have wore their ears out.

Mom and Dad had the wrong phone number and couldn't get hold of me until Wednesday. Mom was in a panic. I couldn't call them since the guest house phone only receives calls. They got the right number from Mary Grey, and we ran up a big phone bill talking. Gabe and Tim are com-ing in February. They've been trying to get tickets. The ministry at Cane Creek is still exploding. They are building a big office and storehouse out in the yard. God moves in mysterious ways. Two years ago we were just an ordinary country family hoeing beans.

We had a good week in town, but it's also nice to be back. The whole village, plus Awongs folks, came down to meet the plane Monday. So they opened three more crates and carried them up. Now I've a total of six up here. It was fun to go through them yesterday. I didn't realize how tired I was of the same seven changes of clothes I brought with me back in July. When I opened my crate of clothes, I cheerfully repacked it with those seven worn out changes, screwed down the lid and sat on it with a grin. Will I ever wear those clothes again?

Monday, standing in Septimas' store with open crates, food supplies, and personal belongings piled around me as people filled their bilams to carry my cargo back to Aikram, I said out loud to myself, "I've got so much stuff!" Rosinda heard me and replied somberly, "You are a very rich lady." For a moment, I really regretted those crates and wished they weren't there. I pray they will not be the cause of any greed or discontent. I don't want to be a stumbling block to these folks. They give and help me freely, and I know they expect me to do the same. After all, I have so much. And truly, I could give a lot with out ever doing without myself. But if they became spoiled and attached to my "riches," what's going to happen when I leave? If America's welfare system completely quit one day, how many dependents would starve to death—in their own, rich, free country? Which is the greater evil, to give too much, or to give nothing? God give me wisdom.

December 26, 1996
"To the praise of the glory of his grace, wherein he hath made us accepted in the beloved." Ephesians 2:6

I'm sitting on a log in the Uwamp meeting house, a 5-6 hour hike from Aikram. There are about 250 Christians from 7 different fellowships here for the four day revival meeting. All of these have been saved in the last nine years since God saved Pastor Allen and he brought the good news back to the people in these mountains. It gives me a thrill to sit here among them and hear the gospel preached in tok ples and hear them sing the Pidgin version of At The Cross. No other white person has been here this deep into the jungle, but the gospel has, and what a change! I was welcomed aggressively as we entered the village. For a moment I felt like I was running the gauntlet. They had all lined up on either side of the trail for about thirty feet, and one of the first I meet flung a wreath of yellow flowers around my neck. Then came the back-beating, hand-shaking, head-rubbing ritual, accompanied by loud singsong welcoming chants. It was enough to terrorize the most liberal Baptist. But I did feel welcome, and it seemed more sincere than the visitor cards they pass out in the States.

The road here was another one of those nightmare trails. I've inched my way across landslides with my face and belly pressed as close to the side of the mountain as I could get. And I've slipped and tripped my way down slime covered logs, and climbed straight up the side of cliffs, but that was the first time I ever waded through the mud and water of the swampy lowlands, fighting mosquitoes and poisonous leeches all the way. At one point, about three hours along, Rosinda said, "Hold your skirt high, the leeches in this area are poisonous and very painful. They will cling to your skirt until they can find your leg." A comforting speech to say the least. I was tempted to climb the nearest tree and stay there, until I remembered the mosquitoes. But I actually made it all the way here without a single leech encounter, and the people are so glad to have me that the trail was worth it.

The preacher Timothy lent his house to Pastor Allen's family, and me, for the weekend, and it's off the ground. Hope I can keep this sore throat under control with vitamin C. Pastor Allen has lost his voice. He is preaching tonight, and since he always yells, his voice usually gets scratchy, but now it's just about gone. He is preaching in a shrill whisper. Well, it is too dark to write, so until later...

December 27, 1996

"And for this cause he is the mediator of the new testament; that by means of death; for the redemption of the transgressions that were under the first testament; they which are called might receive the promise of eternal inheritance."
Hebrews 9:15

Well, we're really packed in here today. Another thirty people showed up, and there are seven on each pew/log now. One busted under the weight of some plump meris perched on it. Sounded like a shotgun going off. I'm wedged in pretty tight myself. The lady on my right is staring unwaveringly at the side of my face, and the kid on my left keeps licking my arm. A would-be cannibal? Us Aikram folks sang John 3:16 in tok ples for a special tonight. The only thing I appreciate about the singing here is the spirit in which they sing, because they sure can't hold a tune. Maybe I could appreciate their consistency.

The preachers are discussing starting two more fellowships in other villages where there are now believers. The gospel is spreading here. Not like wildfire, which is swift and leaves desolation in its path, but like water overflowing the banks of a river in a dry and barren land, slow and sure, saturating and bringing life.

The Sunday-go-to-meeting outfits that are walking around here keep me laughing. One guy is wearing a satin Easter hat minus the flowers. Another is wearing a shirt that is emblazoned with WHITE MEN CAN JUMP! One of the old men is decked out in a pair of pink P.J.s. I've seen a few fancy bathrobes go by too. They're all dressed up in their best.

I can't understand the preaching except for a phrase here and there. It is all in Kumboi, and they are using cheap mikes that blur the clarity of the words. The people seem to be enjoying it though.

I'm rambling now, but it keeps my mind off my back, which is one big knot from sitting so much.

December 30, 1996

"But they that wait upon the Lord shall renew their strength; they shall mount up with wings as eagles: they shall run and not be weary; and they shall walk, and not faint." Isaiah 40:31

This faithful, worn out verse was a prophecy fulfilled today. I quoted it all the way back from the village Uwamp. Sunday afternoon, yesterday, I ate some pork that the folks had mumued. I was violently ill this morning and last night. At 8:30 this morning, still very queasy, but with a stomach so empty it was digesting itself, I set out with Rosinda to come back to Aikram. Back through the swamp of mud, water, and leeches, back up that terrible mountain. I felt like Hannah Hunnard's Much Afraid on her journey to the High Places with Sorrow and Suffering as companions. (Hinds Feet In High Places). At one point in the hike, I had just pulled myself over a particularly steep place and paused on my hands and knees, head hanging as the world tipped and spun in the most delightful manner, and suddenly Satan was there beside me: "Look at yourself," says he (in my mind) "you look, feel, and smell like death warmed over. Here you are out in the middle of the jungle on a tiny island and so sick you can't even stand up. Poor you. Nobody knows and nobody cares. Who's going to get saved out of this experience? You are suffering for no reason at all. It's all in vain." Now if he had stuck to the pity party I would have been quite willing to listen, but that last phrase, "all in vain," was such an outrageous lie that I actually laughed out loud. The people with me turned to stare at me in concern. Perhaps they thought I was vomiting again. "No," I said to Satan, "It is not in vain. If no one ever got saved on this island from here on out, it would still not be in vain, because every weary, miserable step I take says much louder than words ever could, "My God is worthy." And oh, He's worthy of this and so much more. I cannot be sick enough, tired enough, or miserable enough to give Him the glory He deserves. Then suddenly, my Lord was there with me and I felt His love and appreciation wash over me. I was just as sick and weak, but I was filled and overflowing with the joy of the Lord. I would not have traded places with anyone on earth at that moment. For I knew that the One I had sought to please, was very pleased. I knew that I was giving Him glory, and He deeply appreciated it. And I understood for the first time how other Christians who have suffered untold agonies, could do so with courage and joy. And I knew that they are to be envied, not pitied.

Rosinda saw that I was faint from the lack of protein. She took the short cut across the landslides at a run (an incredible feat, or should I say feet?)

to get for me some beef crackers out of my storeroom. Old Bill, who had been left behind as guardian protector of the home-front, looked out of his hut and saw that my storage room door was open. He came running across as fast as his feeble legs would take him, brandishing an ax and giving a war hoop that betrayed the pastime of his younger days. I've no doubt he was disappointed to discover it was only Rosinda on a rescue mission. She returned by the main path and met us on the near side of Fogefoge, two hours walk from Aikram. The protein and salt revived me enough to make it the rest of the way, and now I don't feel so bad at all.

The bung (meeting) at Uwamp went well I think. Sunday morning, about twenty unsaved folks showed up, and we filled the aisles and the ground around the speaker. There was an old man present that was always reverently and lovingly addressed as 'Basunt' (grandfather). They told me that he had been a terrible sinner. He had three wives and twenty some-thing children when he heard the gospel and got saved. It so changed him that soon all his children and wives were saved and most of his boys are now preachers and pastors. His daughters are all pastors' wives. His whole focus in life is to tell the gospel, and you can count on him being at every revival, aggressively seeking out and sharing his testimony to any unbeliev-er. There is always a crowd around him listening as he waves his arms and beats his chest, and often his listeners, while preaching about Jesus. Pastor Allen said, "If every Christian were like our faithful Basunt there would be no heathen left in P.N.G.."

One morning, some of the pastors of the other fellowships came over to sit and talk with Allen. Rufus and Allen have both been out to Bible school and know some English. Rufus said he had heard that I am Jewish and wanted to know what Israel was like. I explained that my great-great grandparents had come to America before the Holocaust and that I had never seen Israel myself. "What's the Holocaust?" Assuming they were only unfamiliar with the word, I briefly stated that it was the cause of the II World War when Hitler killed millions of Jews. They stopped eating and began to question me with intensity, saying, "Why have we never heard about this? We knew there was a war, but we never heard about Hitler." I gave them some dates and details, telling about the concentration camps and incinerators. Excitedly, they told me to go home and write it all down clearly for them to study so they could preach about it. Bible school grads, the two most educated men in these mountains, never heard of the Ho-locaust. I think I'll write home for a simple book on the subject and see if Dad has written anything about the prophecies involved. Too bad Dad isn't

here to preach a class on Jewish history and prophecy. They would love
it. They'd love a class on anything beyond the bare essentials. They have
stayed so long on the foundations of faith that they're ready for some meat
to chew. Again I say, a Bible school is the heart of God's plans here. I look
forward to seeing it happen and the inevitable results.

January 7, 1997

*"Who will rise up for me against the evil doers? Or who will stand up for me
against the workers of iniquity? Unless the LORD had been my help, my soul
had almost dwelt in silence." Psalm 94:16-17*

Nathan did a phone patch and talked to me last Tuesday. He will be
coming with Tim instead of Gabe. I painted all weekend and got the under-
coat on all the doors, windows, tables, and chairs. It rained all last week
too. One night there was a storm, and after everything was completely
soaked, the winds came. It demolished my cookhouse and blew the tin
off the church-house and several people lost their roofs. There are banana
trees laying every where. Nobody slept much either. It sounded like one
continuous tornado. There have been several small earth tremors lately
too. Rainy season is definitely here.

Sunday afternoon everyone decided to go down and carry crates and
food up on Monday. I went with them and we stayed the night at Fogefoge. The smoke nearly killed me. I spent every moment I could outside
under the house. How they can gaze, eyes wide open, into a cloud of acrid
smoke is beyond me. Some of the Kongorau folks also joined us, and we
left at daybreak for Kenainj. There were about twenty people in all. We
got half the food stuffs and six crates. There are only two crates left, and
the food. Another trip will get it all. We all carried as much as we could,
me included, and were exhausted by the time we reached Aikram again.
I handed Jerry forty kina to give to the church at Kongorau, and fifty for
Rock Baptist. All day I had felt uneasy and prayed continuously throughout
the day for wisdom as to how much to give the Aikram folks. I asked God
to protect them from covetousness. They had said they were working for
free, but I was still uneasy. That evening Priscilla came to talk to me and
looked both worried and ashamed. She said Pastor Allen was too ashamed
to come talk to me and sent her instead. She had in her hand the fifty kina
I had given Jerry earlier and a letter that the Aikram folks had dictated.
They said they reject the fifty kina because it is not enough. They said they
have worked hard for me for six months now, and I haven't done anything
to pay them, and this fifty kina is an insult. They say they want thirty kina

per crate and some for building my house, which adds up to be K480.00, or they will never help me in any way again. They were pretty riled and complaining. It was mostly Tomby, Jashun, Ben, and their wives, and some of the girls too. Pastor Allen was surprised, because the original understanding was that Christians help Christians without charge. He told them that if they demand pay here, they will not receive reward in Heaven. They got angry with him and said that if he didn't cooperate with them they would stop coming to church and never help him again either. And as I sat there listening to Priscilla, the words seemed like blows, but they weren't unexpected blows. I guess God had been preparing me for it all day. In fact, it was a relief just to know what was going on and what they expected. Priscilla was angry to the point of tears and there was a bitter smugness in her voice as she said, "Now you see what they are really like. On the outside they smile and call you daughter; on the inside they are angry and greedy. When I first came, I thought they loved me too, but you can never give enough to satisfy them, they'll always want more. And they'll always talk behind your back."

I saw then the reason for the chasm, the rift between her and Allen's people. In the very beginning, when they treated her like this, she withdrew her soul from loving them, and they in turn continue to bite back. Now they're ready to start all over with me. The Spirit said, "Be careful what you say now." So I paused and thought and prayed a split instant before I answered her, and God gave me the right words, and yes, the right heart. I knew somehow that the rest of my ministry here hinged on my reaction to this. "I am not angry with them, Priscilla. I love them. I am surprised and hurt that it is my money they like and not me, but I am not going to stop loving them. God did not withhold His only Son from ungrateful humanity, and He does not love us because we are worthy. Tell them I don't have that much money right now, but when Nathan comes I will pay them K550.00 for all the work they have done for me in the last six months." She was still angry and said I should refuse to pay them anything and never give anything to them again.

Pastor Allen told them what I said, and they are willing to wait, although they won't be doing anything for me in the meantime. I am not entirely above it all. I feel somehow that it is my fault for not offering to pay sooner, even if they did claim to being doing it free. They do deserve to be paid, for they have worked hard for me. The blow comes in knowing that they are not real. That they smile and call me daughter, when inside they are angry and hateful. But at last I can see clearly what is going on. I can see Satan and his ultimate failure, and the hand of God and His ultimate victory.

Just now a bunch of the girls and Waina came on the pretense of looking at my photo albums. Their faces were watchful for any lack of acceptance or welcome on my part. Like a child who has done it's best to be unlovable and then fears he has succeeded. Once they were convinced that I am not angry or depressed, they left. Thank you, God, for being my strong tower and refuge from the storm.

January 11, 1997

"Yet a man is born unto trouble, as the sparks fly upward. I would seek unto God, and unto God would I commit my cause:Which doeth great things and unsearchable; marvelous things without number... To set up on high those that be low; that those which mourn may be exalted to safety." Job 5:7,8,9,11

Saturday morning.

I don't have the strength to do much else but write. It has been a while since I fasted, and my body is not used to it. I have lost ten pounds in the last two days. No doubt, I'll gain it all back this evening when I break my fast. I have that meal planned down to the last grain of salt! Steven is outside banging around, trying to put the screen wire on my windows. Everything has been painted but one chair. I was going to do that today, but I ran out of energy. All is well in the village. Priscilla comes to visit just about every night. For nine years she has been without a friend with whom she could talk to honestly, and now she's about to smother me with gratitude for just liking her. Anna is mad at me lately. I don't know what about. But Anna is always mad at somebody. I don't think she's saved yet. Rosilla, Alice, and Rosinda come by to visit fairly often too. I haven't figured Rosinda out yet. I have spent more time with her than with anybody here, but I know her least of all. The best way to describe her is, uninvolved. She doesn't say what she thinks, never gives an opinion or tells about when she was younger. She avoids deep subjects entirely, and anytime I want to know what's been going on (who died, what did she do today, etc.) I have to drag it out of her. My books keep her coming back. She loves to read. She read my Children's Illustrated Bible Stories from cover to cover. It's about a 6th grade level and one and a half inches thick. Now she's half way through Don Richardson's Peace Child, and loving it. I spoke her name while she was reading yesterday, and she jumped in her seat, explaining sheepishly, "It's written to frighten me. I'm going to dream about cannibals eating me." If you can read English, you can go anywhere, be anybody, and do anything.

Pastor Allen has gone to Kongorau. He has refused to preach for the Ai-kram folks lately. I guess he's discouraged. He says he preaches three times a week and they never learn or change. He says they still act like heathens and he's sick of preaching to them. I have to admit, I'd hate to be a pastor in P.N.G..

Rufus came yesterday. He said he wants me to write home to the Churches in the U.S. and request that they send a man to start a Bible school here in the mountains for all the preacher boys. I have not mentioned my vision for a Bible school to them, but God is speaking. Rufus said he'd like to help teach. If someone did come, he could begin teaching immediately, in English, to a handful of preacher boys that speak English. There'd be Rufus, Allen, Frank, Benson, Peter, and maybe Lawrence and Timothy. You'd have to go slow and repeat a lot, but a pastor's class, two or three times a week for a year, while studying Pidgin, would be extremely profitable. By the time you knew Pidgin, you'd already have a handful of national teachers who had all the doctrinal kinks worked out of them. You could teach them the basics: Bible history, authority, repentance, baptism, NT Church, etc. Soon they'd be ready to teach as well. Oh, man! I get excited just thinking about it. God, send us a man to do this job! There are too many local languages involved to teach in anything but Pidgin, using the Pidgin and English KJV New Testament. And then there are the boys like Luke. A real man of God in the making, a leader in the mold, who cannot read a single word. A literacy class would be a necessity. A simple history and geography class would be profitable too, just to tie Bible events and places together. Will it happen, Lord? I'm praying my heart out for it.

January 18, 1997
"For our light affliction, which is but for a moment, worketh for us a far more exceeding weight of glory." II Corinthians 4:17

What a lovely verse! "Exceeding weight of glory." God's promises are not small. It has been a quiet week until yesterday, so there hasn't been much to write about. Yesterday morning, Priscilla came to return a pen, and I was so absorbed in my studies that I hardly looked up. But for once she seemed in a hurry, dropping the pen on the table and keeping her face down as she turned to leave. On impulse, I asked with real concern as she drew abreast of the door, "Are you all right?" Whereupon she burst into sobs, and I jumped up to lead her back to a chair. She cried for a while, and I hovered at her shoulder worriedly. I never know what to do when people burst into tears, not being prone that way myself. So I hovered, and she cried. Until she finally got control, I simply waited in silence.

First she apologized profusely for crying, then came the story. Allen
went to Fogefoge yesterday, and when he returned she did not have his din-
ner cooked. They argued. The result being, he told her to pack her bags and
leave him and the boys for good. She begged him to let her stay and threatened to tell everybody he was making her leave. He called her some names
they use in Simbai that are worse than anything English has come up with.
She ran out into the night crying, and he bolted the door behind her. After
wandering around in the rain for a while she came back and knocked at the
door. An hour later he let her in. This morning she wanted to go to Fogefoge to be alone, but he forbade her, and then she came to return my pen.
Whether she had expected to talk or not, I don't know. She said this is the
sixth time in the last year he has demanded that she leave. I asked her why,
and she said she doesn't know; he won't tell her why. Now I know marriage
squabbles are never 100% one party's fault, and so I kept asking questions.
But all she would say is, "I don't know, I don't understand. He wasn't always
like this, what is wrong? I love him, I don't want to leave." She begged me
not to tell anybody, saying that no one here knows he wants her to leave.
She said if they knew he wanted to send her away they would be very angry
with him and not let him preach, and then he would hate her forever. In this
culture, if a man rejects his wife, his family has to pay the bride price again
and pay for every child born of that union. So rejecting Priscilla would cost
his folks a lot of money. She threatened him that if he insists on sending her
away, she is going to tell everybody the real story and make sure they know
she is not deserting him, but that he is forcing her to leave. So now he's
madder than ever, but afraid that he could lose his position here.

I knew Pastor Allen was no angel, but I didn't know his problems were
this serious. He can't have always been this way, because God has obviously
used him in the past, and Priscilla would never have married him in the
first place. It must be the work of Satan to destroy the foundations. I began
fasting and praying for them yesterday when she told me, and even walked
around their house rebuking Satan. Only baby Noah saw me. I don't know
what condition he's in now, but I'm praying for full repentance toward
God in both their lives. It will only stay judgment for a brief while if he
allows her to stay for fear of losing his prominence. If he could recognize
it as the work of Satan and stand against it, the battle would be won. So, I
shall have to write the end of this story later. I hope they get it worked out
before I starve to death.

Well, Priscilla came a while ago to buy rice and tin meat and told me
that Pastor Allen stayed mad all day yesterday, refusing to let her cook or

eat in their house. While he was sleeping in the afternoon, she cooked his food and brought it to him, expecting him to refuse it. But he ate and told her that they needed to talk and pray. That evening he apologized and prayed and confessed to God and asked her to stay. She said, "So, everything is a bit all right, but not really." I think it's still tense and edgy. He is struggling with pride, she with forgiveness. I broke my fast in thanksgiving for answered prayer. But the battle is not over yet. Satan is quick to retreat, but only to advance on another side.

Still the same day, 10:00 P.M.

Priscilla was here all evening singing with me. My song book, with all the songs I've written since I came, was on the table, and she asked about it. I explained that when God teaches me something new, He often gives me a song with it. She looked through the book and stopped at the song True Love, which I wrote this week. She requested that I sing it. The words are as follows:

True Love
Chorus:
True love, Real love,
Love without a limit
Love without pride in it.
It was True love.
(1)
To the garden alone the Lord had come
There he knelt and prayed to God above
"Not my will be done,
But thine," said the Son
It was True Love.
(2)
Upon a hill there stood a rugged tree
And dark as night the heavens were above
For crimson was the stream
That flowed for you and me
It was True love.
(3)
Mary found the stone was rolled aside
The grave could not hold the King of Love
Death had lost to Life
And we serve a Risen Christ
It was True Love.

When I finished, there were tears in her eyes, and she repeated to herself, "Love without pride in it." Then confessed, she said, "I don't really love my husband. God has given you this song for me. It has reminded me that true love is without pride and without limit. Jesus did not love us because we were good to Him. It was true love when He died." And she sat there repeating the chorus as if her life, or perhaps her marriage, depended on it. It was a lesson for me too. It is odd that a person can write a song and still not get the full extent of it's meaning, but there was also a message for me in that phrase, "Love without pride in it." Is there anybody on earth that I love without a shred of pride? Do I even love God that way? How very humbling that the Creator of the universe, God Almighty, should love us that way.

As she left, I said, "See you at service tomorrow." Worriedly, she replied, "I don't know. Maybe. Pastor packed all my clothes in a suitcase and locked it and hid the key." Then I noticed she was wearing the laplap that usually serves as a curtain. Sweet, mature, adorable Pastor Allen!

January 22, 1997

"Now thanks be to God, which always causeth us to triumph in Christ, and maketh manifest the savour of his knowledge by us in every place."
II Corinthians 2:14

Thursday evening.

Allen and his family have gone to Kongorau for a week. We got news that his brother Peter and family, who has been attending Bible school in Lae, will be coming by plane tomorrow. Rosinda's brother Frank is coming too, and most of the community here went down to Kenainj to meet them. Rosinda stayed behind to watch all the kids—and me. I went down to the water to wash clothes and take a bath, and when I returned, Papa Amblinch was here waiting for me with another man by the name of Kuli. Amblinch is a friendly old man that comes by about once every two weeks with a bag full of pineapples, bananas, and peanuts, which he gives to me cheerfully, saying, "Yu pikinini bilong mi. Mi no ken lusim yu." (You're my child, I can't abandon you.) He stays until I feed him, and then ambles off with a promise to return. Lately he brings someone with him. He is not a Christian and not from this village, but claims to be Seventh Day Adventist. Today the man he brought, David Kuli, had a special message. He said in Pidgin, "We want a missionary in our village too. We want one this year, not next year. We like people like you so you can ring America up on your radio and tell them to send us one right away." We talked about it a while,

and I discovered that his village is Kondol, close to Aiome, a day or more
away. Their dialect is of the Kalam/Kumboi family, and is called Fungun.
He spoke and understood this dialect in Aikram (Yimbe Munum) as well. I
said I'd do my best for him and suggested he come back and talk to Nathan
and Tim when they are here. Then I told him that Jesus is coming soon and
asked, "Yu stap redi, o nogat?" (are you ready?) He answered in Pidgin,
"It is good for us to go to church, then we'll be ready. But everybody
has different churches now, Anglican, S.D.A, Nazarene, E.B.C., Baptist;
which one is right? I don't know. Which one do you believe?" I said that
I meet with the Baptist here in Aikram, but went on, "It is good to go to
church and to sing songs and be happy, but it is not enough. Anglican is not
enough, S.D.A. is not enough, Baptist is not enough—only Jesus—He is
enough." Then, in my limited Pidgin, I gave the gospel and was thrilled just
to be able to witness again and be understood. Kuli shook his head when
I finished, "Your talk is true in my ears. It beats what all the others say. I
know that you are not lying and I want to hear more." Now, I know his
response was partly because he wanted to get on my good side so I'd help
him get a missionary, but what more could you expect from an unbeliever?
Only the Christian desires God with a sincere heart, the unbeliever doesn't
even know what he's asking for. He had material wealth in mind, but there
were no closed doors to spiritual wealth either. He told me to send him
word by Amblinch of the date Nathan will be here, so he can come talk to
him as well. I fed them a big meal, and after they ate, they left.

Rosinda and Jesse and Sisilya were here all day too. This afternoon, I got
out color crayons and paper for them. They just sat staring at it, even after
Rosinda explained what they should do. A six-year-old and a four-year-old
who have never colored a picture! Finally, I joined them on the floor and
started my own drawing. After watching me a while, they tentatively made
scribbles in the corner of their paper. Rosinda joined us, and soon there
were four of us, big girls and little, laughing and coloring away. They carried their pictures and mine home with them. It was a fun, profitable day.

Tomorrow, if it is not raining, I may hike up to Fogefoge for some rose
cuttings to plant around the house. Roses really grow well here, and I des-
perately need exercise. All I do is SIT. I'm afraid I shall eventually turn into
one big butt if I don't get out and move around.

January 23, 1997

"The LORD hath appeared of old unto me saying yea, I have loved thee with an everlasting love: therefore with lovingkindness have I drawn thee."
Jeremiah 31:3

Allen's brother Peter and his wife and three children plus Frank all came today from Lae. I guess they have come to stay. Frank looks pretty fat to have been sick and in the hospital. Before he even went on into the village to greet his family, he wanted to go in and see my house. With the air of a statesman viewing a sky-rise erected in his honor, he said in his best English, "Hmm, development." I had to laugh.

I studied until eleven, but the sun was out, and it had been so long since I had seen it, that I just had to go outside. For the next three hours I worked like a mad-woman, making a new garden for lettuce, carrots, and radishes. Then Rosinda and the kids came (she generally has a flock of kids around her), and we overhauled the outside entirely: Flower beds, onion beds, a longer rock walk, and gravel and rocks in front of my rain tanks. It looks great, and I am cheered up to have had some exercise. I want to make another raised bed tomorrow for sage and mint. We planted pink and white roses all around the house, about eighteen cuttings. We also planted yellow orchids, Nasturtiums, Statice, and a few more I don't know the names of. My four avocado trees are coming up nicely at the corners of the house, and I have planted a small bushy pine about every ten feet apart around the perimeter as well. The flowers are planted in beds between the pines. It should look beautiful around here in about six months to a year.

Septimas was gone to the bush this week, so the girls were unable to get my mail or post any. It has been so long since I heard from home!

January 25, 1997

"Oh give thanks unto the LORD for he is good, because his mercy endureth forever." Psalm 118:1

The girls just left, all eight of them, Rosinda, Rosilla, Alice, Lioni, Anna, Julian, Lucy, and Stella. Only Jenny was too busy to come. For the last few nights we have been having music lessons. I decided to work on their rhythm first, since it is the most obvious fault in the singing here. To be honest, I expected zero success with the venture, but they have come through with shining colors. I had them beat on the table or floor with their palms in four-four timing, all together, while counting out loud, "one, two, three, four." The first night, only two of them stayed with me, and the rest just pounded at random. It sounded more like rain on the roof than rhythm. But they went home and practiced, and the next night everybody but Anna could count and beat the table at the same time. Then I started strumming the guitar in four-four timing and counting out loud so they could associate the strum of the guitar to the rhythm they were pounding. It was then that the idea of timing suddenly dawned on them and they realized that music has its own built-in conductor. While they counted and I strummed, I sang God is so Good, counted, sang and then made them sing while I counted. They were delighted with the effect. For the first time ever, they were all singing in one accord. Tonight, even Anna had figured it out, and we practiced God is so Good for a special on Sunday in Pidgin, English, and tok ples. Somehow the timing has helped them stay on key better too, or maybe it's the guitar, I don't know, but everybody is pleased with the results.

I got a message from CRMF that my folks have been trying to get through (phone patch) but haven't been able so they sent a fax to CRMF and they read it to me over the radio. It said that Nathan and Tim will be here February 5th. Just ten days! I was tickled to get that message, but I still need to talk to them. Maybe I'll have to try and make a phone patch from this end.

I've got bread and eggs and mail down at the airstrip rotting. Septimas is gone to the bush and it's locked up in his store for over a month now. I hope somebody will go down and get it for me Monday, but they probably won't, so maybe I'll go on Tuesday or Wednesday, depending on the weather. Who knows? It's an awfully long, miserable hike. Time for bed.

January 30, 1997
"And this is life eternal, that they might know thee the only true God, and Jesus Christ whom thou hast sent." John 17:3

Thursday morning.

This week is going quickly. Monday, after studies, I worked outside and inside cleaning. Tuesday it rained all day, and I just studied. Yesterday was Wednesday, and I walked to Kenainj and back for my mail, bread, and eggs. The folks here don't plan to walk another step till they get paid, so it was up to me. Rosinda went with me though, and because she was scared, she asked Luke to come along too, which he did. I am glad he did, because we passed some creepy looking people. Luke would be a blessing to any society, no matter what his color, culture, language, or race. He's just one of those people. He has no father (bush baby), and so has learned to work very hard, which is unusual for the boys in this area. Luke enjoys helping people. He keeps me a stack of dry wood split and stacked, without being asked, and does the same for Priscilla and some of the others. About four months ago he came to this village, heard the gospel, and was saved. He's only fifteen or sixteen years old right now, but I believe God is going to use him in the future. I pray for him all the time.

Anyway, our trip to Kenainj. They, Rosinda and Luke, made me go first so I could set the pace, but that early in the morning, no one has been on the trails yet and there are spider webs spun across the path about every six feet in some places. And, they are all face high. But I have to watch my feet since I'm usually balancing on a slippery log and, considering the drop, I can't afford to fall. Therefore, I get plastered with one web after another. By the time we reached Sakup I looked like a saint of old, glittering with the glory of a resurrection not yet fully realized. A thousand silver strands, still wet with the night's dew, webbed my face like a florescent cocoon. I refused to wonder where the spiders might be!

At the airstrip, the plane arrived just before we did and brought another box of mail, bread, and eggs. Septimas was still in the bush, but David, the MAF agent had come the day before and had a key to the store. The first box had been there over a month, and I never found out about it, so everything was rotten but the mail. We carried the fresh box, which arrived just before we did, and a container of kerosene back. God blessed us with good weather all the way, and we made it in just over nine hours this time (we took several shortcuts). The best I can figure, it's about 30 miles round trip. Takes a few years off my life every time I try it. My muscles are adjusted now, but my feet! I felt like I was walking on bloody stumps by the time we arrived at Aikram. Idioms like "last leg of the journey" began to make sense.

Well, Tim and Nathan left America last night and should be in L.A right now.

Priscilla came last night to ask for Pastor Allen if he could borrow money to buy a ticket to Madang. That is the second time he has asked. I again said no. Partly because I don't have it to spare, partly because borrowing and lending always leads to grief, and partly because if I did, he'd want to borrow money every other week. Then I'd have a bigger problem. So he's going to ask his brother Peter for it. That's all for now; time to study.

February 4, 1997

"...for he hath said, I will never leave thee nor forsake thee. So that we may boldly say; The Lord is my helper and I will not fear what man shall do unto me." Hebrews 13:5,6

Two promises there: #1) He'll never leave me. #2) Man shall do unto me!

This is Tuesday afternoon. I've been fasting for three days and broke my fast this morning. Sunday I was kind of down. Sundays are the loneliest days for me. I can't study; I do that all week. My house is clean; I do that on Saturday. I can play the guitar, and usually do at least four hours, but there is still a few hours left that I just stand in the middle of the floor and say out loud in frustration, "God, I need somebody to talk to!" I go visit the Aikram folks, and although we can communicate somewhat now, there's no common ground to talk about. It's not a miserable sort of loneliness, because I often laugh at myself for talking out loud and pacing the floor, but it is frustrating and boring. Often, at those times, God will give me a song. I'll be reading the Bible, and a story and tune just seem to leap out at me, and soon I'll be playing and singing it like I've known it all my life. There are now 19 songs in my Songs From the End of the Earth song book. I add one about every other week. Sunday, He gave me a song called I'll Walk Upon the Waves. It's about Peter walking with Jesus on the water. I always learn something from the songs He gives me. They're my tangible stepping-stones of faith.

To change the subject, Luke dug a toilet hole for me yesterday. It's about 10 feet deep and 4 ½ feet square. It's funny, but the day before, I had despaired of ever having my own outhouse (I heard Pastor Allen and the men discussing where they could put the community toilet so that it would be accessible to me too). After alternating for a few hours between mad, despair, and determination, I finally gave my non-existent outhouse to God. "God," says I "you can have my toilet. I don't mind peeing in a bucket the rest of my life." And I forthwith forgot all about it. The next morning, Luke met me at the door with a shovel, "Where do you want your toilet?" he asked. I laughed like he'd said something funny, and he looked confused. "Anywhere!" I said and laughed again. That's my God. He knows every hair on my head and every toilet hole in P.N.G..

Later in the afternoon, Luke came and asked me nervously, in a low voice so no one could hear, "Plis, bai yu skulim mi long ridim Baibel?" (Please, would you teach me how to read the Bible?) It's hard to explain how you feel at times like that. It's like hearing somebody ask, "Please, I want to get saved, would you tell me how?" You want to laugh, cry, and do cartwheels all at the same time. Of course, I said yes. Watching him dig the toilet hole that afternoon, I had stood at my window and prayed for him, prayed that God would preserve him in integrity, make him a future leader for these people, and somehow teach him how to read. God put the answer for that prayer in my lap. I made a primer starting with all the vowels in Pidgin, going on to the consonants and simple words. I decorated it with color crayons and wrote his name on it. He came around 6 P.M. and sweated and fidgeted over those five vowels like his life was at stake. Finally it seemed to make sense and he chanted them faster and faster, "A - Papa, E - Belo, I - liklik, O - dok, U - dua!" Then he confessed, "It's really hard, but I'm going to pray really hard too, and God will teach me how to read." "You bet he will, Luke. And I'm praying too." I sent the primer, paper, and pencil home with him to study and copy the vowels over and over. He went out the door with his head held high and an almost indiscernible whisper, "A - Papa, E - Belo..."

Well, to change subjects once again, I received a radio message today from Kenainj that somebody named Nathan had arrived and wanted us to come pick him up. The message doesn't make sense, because even if I could "pick him up," I couldn't carry him five hours back to the village! Seriously though, I guess maybe they came to Kenainj airstrip this morning and there was nobody to meet them. But Nathan knows the way here, so maybe they're walking this way even now. I cooked a big meal and made two pallets. I am expecting them any minute. I think some of the Aikram folks went to meet them on the way. Until later...

February 10, 1997
"Thanks be unto God for his unspeakable gift." II Corinthians 9:15

Nathan and Tim did arrive even as I wrote the last word of that last entry. Nathan stopped beneath my window and called out "Ay yande" (my sister) with a very bad accent, and I squealed with surprise. This is exactly one week later and they have done everything they could do as far as carpentry and wiring in that period of time. I have beds, book shelves, couch, desk, clothesline, toilet, and camp shower. Also a computer and printer. No more diary by hand. I've been trying to type everything I've written since last October. It is going to take a while, but I want to mail the floppy to my folks when we go to town next week. Tim got a case of culture shock and left this afternoon in hopes of catching a plane tomorrow. We had to hold him down every time a plane flew over. He wasn't scared or anything, just ready to go home.

I paid the Aikram bunch the money they asked for and gave Pastor Allen a love offering. I haven't heard any mention of them going to get the last two crates and food. They are glad to have Nathan back and were impressed with Tim. Allen was trying to leave for Madang when they came in on the plane he was waiting for, so he changed his mind and came back with them. He left with Tim this afternoon. They had a conference (all the men and Tim and Nathan) and said that they have a problem with me not being married. They want a male missionary, and told Tim to look for a husband for me. He said he'd do what he could.

Dad sent a tape on the authority of the believer, concerning prayer, and it was a great encouragement. As I told them in a letter home, I almost believe God's main purpose in sending me here was so I could pray for other laborers for the Bible school. And I know without a doubt, as surely as I know my own name, that He has answered those prayers and there is someone on the way. This Bible school is the heartbeat of what God plans to do here. It is only a matter of time.

Cathy phone patched and said she is coming in March. Who knows? Nathan and I plan to go out to town next week. I don't need groceries, but I do need a break. We'll swim, see the sights, and maybe even go to Lae for a few days. Then he'll be off to Laos to see T. J., and I'll go back to Aikram to study language.

February 13, 1997

"Now unto the King eternal, immortal, invisible, the only wise God, be honour and glory for ever and ever. Amen." I Timothy 1:17

I just finished typing all the handwritten entries I've made since October, 1996, and decided to go on and type another entry. It is great having a computer again.

This is Thursday. Tim could not get a flight out last week, and walked down again on Tuesday with Pastor Allen to try again. The plane came yesterday, and they both left for Madang. Tim may be in Moresby by now. Nathan has been reading my book on the life of Josephus, the Roman/Jew historian. We both have been fasting since yesterday morning. I told him I usually do every other week and he decided to try it with me. Twenty-four hours later he is miserable and claims he'll never fast again. My language studies have been completely neglected since Nathan and Tim came. I only missed one day the whole month of January, but it looks as if I may miss the whole month of February. But I intend to enjoy the company while I've got it.

A man in lower Aikram died last night and there are streams of people going by with their faces painted with the white mourning mud. They look like throngs of the dead themselves. The man was Awong's brother, and he was not saved, although Pastor Allen and Jerry had witnessed to him many times. He went to the witch doctor's in Lae, and they told him he had a big mushroom growing inside of him and would die, then he went to a regular doctor who said he had cancer and about one month to live. So he came home to die two weeks ago.

That's all the news for now.

February 26, 1997
"Before the mountains were brought forth, or ever thou hadst formed the earth and the world, even from everlasting to everlasting, thou art God."
Psalm 90:2

I just returned from Madang about two hours ago and don't have the energy to do much of anything but type. It was a good week in all. We got stuck on the airstrip for the usual two days waiting for the weather to clear and the plane to come. When we were finally in the air, I told the pilot that if I'd had a cannon I would have blown him out of the air the day before when he flew over and decided not to land because of the weather. Madang was a little cooler this time, which was pleasant, and I didn't have to walk around buying supplies. Nathan and I had planned to rent a car and drive to Lae for a few days, but it turned out that it would cost K800 to rent a car for five days, so we just stayed in Madang. We found a man with a boat that took us out to Jais Aben (a diving resort) two different times. There is hardly ever anybody there swimming, and we enjoyed spending the days paddling from island to island and viewing the coral and tropical fish. We received a fax and phone call from Mom and Dad during the week. Tim had brought home a letter from Pastor Allen, and they were pretty alarmed. I think I shall copy the letter here. It is exactly as written from Pastor Allen to Dad.

> Dear pastor Michael,
>
> Grace in Jesus Name and Peace from God our Father and the blessed Holy Spirit may bless your spiritual heart. First of all I would like to thank thee for the very encouraging letter which I have received on the 5th of February by Tim and Nathan.
>
> The Rock Baptist Church also thanks thee Cane Creek Baptist for K550 for their labor. And I also thank thee K50 for your

church love offering to me. Blessed it to give than to receive.
Not forgetting Rock Baptist is still praying for Cane Creek
Baptist.

We are far from the body but we are together in Spirit. We
Christians are spiritually fine with Rebekah, But the biggest
problems we are facing now, Rebekah is not married. The 3
community's (1) Aikulan, 2 waibai, 3 Kinnal Strongly talk to me
that if is married than she can get our language. If not she may
get back to state or America. I was try to talk over her but she
told me that I must not interfere with her ministry so I have no
time to talk over with her. They also told my Church members
not to work with her learning their tongue. (Komboi)

Pastor Michael, The Devil is working very hard so it very
hard for me to keep your daughter safely at Aikulan Vilage. They
also said to me, if you Pastor not listen to us than she has to pay
some large amount of money like K50 or hundred thousand before she can learn out Kumboi tongue. They said if the payment
is not done then she has to leave the country.

Pastor Michael I believe this is not the will of the Lord so she
has to go back to the country before may or June 1997. Another
thing P.N.G. general election is coming up on the May and June
of this year so for the safety she has to go back by May or June
of this year 1997.

Pastor and Cane Creek Baptist Church this is all I have to
share with you all.

Keep on saving the living God preach the Word and Reach
the Lost. Thats all see you all in Rapture.

Pastor Allen Gami Akiz

So that is Allen's letter to Dad. It is not surprising that it had them worried. It was a bit of a blow to me too. However, knowing pastor Allen, I
know that the situation is not quite as extreme as he made it sound. The
two villages that he mentioned, other than Aikram (Aikulan), I have never
even heard of, so they can't be close or prominent. Also, he has never tried
to talk to me on the subject, and if he had, I would never have told him
to mind his own business. However, I'm not guiltless because I know that
my attitude towards him probably caused him to say what he did. When it
comes to loving and appreciating pastor Allen, I'm a miserable failure. I get
along great with every single person up here except him. He can't stand

me either, and has finally decided that he'd rather not have me at all, and so
is trying to get rid of me. Of course, if America was willing to pay a hundred thousand kina to keep me here, then he could endure me a little longer. I know it is my fault for not showing more respect and honor towards
his position. I am tempted to say I tried my hardest, but I know I really
didn't. He's the opposite of everything I admire and respect in a man, and
I'm a terrible pretender, and pretty critical too—especially when it comes
to leadership that lacks integrity. It is also their culture. He, and the others,
can't stand seeing a woman in control of material wealth and money. It is
opposite of everything they were used to. So I can't blame him for being
fed up with me. He never really expected or wanted a Bible in his own
language, and wouldn't use it if he had it. It was the money and prestige
that prompted their invitation for me to come here. And they haven't
gained either. So they want a man, or a hundred thousand kina. I could be
depressed and defeated, but instead I am excited and glad. Why? Because
I know that God is preparing them for the coming of a man to teach the
Bible school. They have asked for it and now even demanded it, so when he
comes, they'll be more apt to accept and listen to him. Of course, it wasn't
in God's plan for me to rile Allen, but it isn't such a catastrophe as Satan
meant it to be. And I shall strive harder, yea, give it my best to treat him
according to his position, not his character. He mentioned that I should
leave by May or June, and coincidentally, I will be going home at that time
anyway to speak in several churches and for a large youth conference there
at home. Our church will be flying home T.J. as well. Milton Martin, the
Rogers, the Holland's, Shad Williams, and others will be there to speak and
share. I will stay a few months, and when I return here to Aikram, there
will be someone with me that God has called to teach in the Bible school.
A family or two, but I know there will be someone.

Cathy won't be coming. I talked to her on the phone last night. She is
really depressed and broken sounding. It scares me to think that simply
wavering in your faith can bring on such sadness of soul. It could so easily
be me. I have so many shortcomings that sometimes I tremble and am sure
that soon I shall fall and be set aside permanently from the perfect will
of God. And then He reminds me that He asks for no more than simple
obedience and faith for one moment at a time. He doesn't want me to
face tomorrow while it is yet today. And I find that there is always enough
strength (His supply of course) for the moment at hand. It is only when we
start to dread and plan and fail in the future, that has not even arrived, that

we lose our faith and begin to sink beneath the waves as Peter did. Walking by faith is so simple and easy and—unhuman!

So, the plan is, I stay here until the last week of May, before the election trouble starts (during election time in P.N.G. there is rioting and violence all over the country) and then fly to Moresby where I'll stay and visit Ray and Susanna for a week before flying on to the U.S. I'll stay in America probably 3-6 months, depending on how long it takes to find "The Man." I must confess that I am really looking forward to going home again. These next three months I shall devote to intense Pidgin studies, and tok ples too, although not as concentrated as before. Also I hope to start a literacy class right away, since I managed to find the Kisim Save teaching materials that have alluded me so far. I'd also like to try to tear down the wall I've helped build between Pastor Allen and me, and somehow learn to really love him. God help me!

Walk Upon the Waves

(1)

Once I heard Him call me out by name
I stepped out on the sea with trembling faith
But in the horror of the storm
I soon forgot my Lord
But for His hand, I'd sunk beneath the waves.
Chorus:
But I'm walking with the Master of the sea
Together we have faced the fiercest storms
And no matter how deep the deep
Or perilous the sea
I will walk the waves any day with my Lord.

(2)

Sometimes this world is more than I can take
And the doubts just seem to drown my struggling faith
But in the depths of all my fears
He takes my hand and dries my tears
And I rise again to walk upon the waves.

(3)

So let the lightening strike, the thunder roll and break
Let the storm howl above me and let it rain
For no matter how deep the sea

Rough the waves beneath my feet,

If my Lord is there, I'll walk upon the waves.

2/2/97

February 28, 1997

"Thanks be unto God for his unspeakable gift." II Corinthians 9:15

Friday afternoon.

I think. Yes, it's Friday. I can't seem to shake this cold, and it has turned into an infection in my head. I reek of garlic, and my stomach stays upset from taking in such large amounts of it. It's bound to kill me, or the infection, eventually. A lot of people in the village are sick with heavy colds, it is so rainy and chilly all the time. Nathan flew to Thailand today and met T.J. in Bangkok. T.J has been on the field one month longer than I have. I wonder how he's doing?

Pastor Allen came hobbling in last night. The plane went to Simbai, since it was too cloudy to land at Kenainj. Allen's knees were so swollen and sore that he went to the "hospital" there at Simbai to get them checked out. They told him that he is allergic to greens and to stop eating them. I never heard of any allergy affecting your joints, but I'm no medical expert either.

Talking about doctors, I think I mentioned the man that died a couple of weeks ago with cancer. His name was Daun, and he was a brother of Papa Ben and Awong. Last week Awong hired a witch from Jimi (the other side of the mountain range) to prophesy and tell who it was that worked magic and killed Daun. The witch used to be a Koi Yimp (a murderer by sorcery), but got a license from the government to practice medicine for money, and now only heals or tells who the murderer is. She has two spirits at her command. Rosinda described them as being like rats, only unseen. They crawl into the sick person's body and find the sickness and eat it, thus healing the person of their disease. Even the Christians here believe in her power, although they won't hire her to heal them. Awong paid her K150.00 to tell who was guilty of killing Daun by sorcery. Nobody dies a natural death in P.N.G.; it's always sorcery. The witch said that it was Papa Abram, an unbeliever from lower Aikram. He wanted to take or buy some of Daun's land a while back, and was refused, and got angry with Daun over it. So he was named as the Koi Yimp, and all of Daun's family demanded that he pay compensation for the murder. He claimed he didn't do it of course, but everyone believes he did, even the Christians. So he brought money and a small pig, but it was refused as not being enough, and negotiations are still going on.

And that is Kumboi culture for you. It is pretty common over all of P.N.G.. I myself believe it is more than culture. There really are demons involved, and you better believe that Satan will take advantage of every situation possible. People really are murdered by sorcery here, maybe not as many as the nationals think, but demons of anger, lust, and violence often possess one body and kill another. There are some people in this area that have gotten saved and testified to having been Koi Yimps (murderers by sorcery) and so they have named the people they killed. Some have been secretly cannibals, also under demonic influence. People that deny demon possession and principalities and powers of the air should come to P.N.G. for a while. It wouldn't take them long to realize who the god of this world is. How thrilling it is to know that *"greater is He that is in us, than he that is in the world."* Satan is just a stepped-on snake with a limited time warranty. His days are numbered.

I haven't studied much at all since coming back. I felt pretty bad the last couple of days and just slept or typed up my songs on the computer. I wrote another one yesterday called Redeem The Time. That makes twenty in my song book.

March 5, 1997

"For a thousand years in thy sight are but as yesterday when it is past, and as a watch in the night." Psalm 90:4

I have to type fast because I don't have much power to work on. The power regulator system Nathan and Tim put in doesn't work. By all appearances, it seemed to, but I finally drained my batteries dry and they weren't recharging. I went without radio, lights or computer for several days. Yesterday I took the regulator apart and put the wires back together, bypassing the regulator system. So the batteries began to recharge and today I had radio contact. But I can't work my computer on the power system and am working off the battery in the computer right now. I may try to charge the solar batteries to their limit and then hook the regulator back up so I can use my computer for a few days. I don't know if that would work or not. It has rained persistently since I got back from Madang.

Boredom just about killed me the first three days. So much time is spent talking, laughing, and doing for other people. With Nathan and Tim gone, I was at a loss to know what to do with myself once again. But now I am back in the groove of talking to myself and staring at the wall in hours of meditation. Knowing that I'm going to go home in just three months makes the days seem so much longer. I've written another two songs this week:

The King was born To Wear a Crown, and He Stands on My Behalf. I won't know if they're any good for a couple of weeks, I never can tell right off.

The rats have been driving me crazy the last few days. I've caught two of them, but there is at least another three, probably five, out to terrorize me. As long as it is light and I can see them they don't bother me. I don't blink an eye when they run over my foot or scurry up the wall in broad daylight. And I gleefully empty the traps of their dead bodies in the morning. But at night, in the oozy black darkness, when one of them gets his feet tangled in my hair and starts swimming frantically like a bug in a whirlpool trying to get out, I have to restrain myself from running out of the house screaming. It's just more than I can take. And they always come out to party at night. The smart ones have survived and intelligently ignore all the delicacies with which I decorate the rat traps. I thought about locking Min-min [dog] in the house with me at night, but she'd make so much noise, not to mention the mess. I should get a cat, but I hate cats almost as much as mice. So what is there left to do? Get up and party with the mice every night and sleep during the day? I am beginning to dread going to bed.

Pastor Allen and I have instituted a truce. He actually came to visit today. I'm being so nice to him that he is beginning to wonder who he is. He and Priscilla are getting along really well lately. He brought her a guitar back from Lae, so she is babying him and cooing over his bad knee. They both look happy and well. His trip to Lae was disappointing for him. Two churches have asked him to come pastor them, but neither have offered any kind of support. He has decided to stay here unless they offer to pay him and give them a place to live. Also, things are progressing here and he is not as discouraged as he was. The man Daun, that died recently, was a big wall between the Christians and the heathen in the other villages. He was a highly respected leader and openly and violently opposed Christianity. He led the attack on the Christians at Fogefoge eight or nine years ago. The church building has been full of unbelievers from other villages the last two weeks since he died. Everyone was afraid to oppose him. The man Abram, that supposedly killed him, has been charged ten thousand kina, ten pigs and ten women for compensation. He has come up with five hundred kina, but all the women in the village ran away for fear of being part of the payment, and the pigs are all still piglets, since the pig killings were just a month ago.

They are beginning to talk about where they are going to put the Bible school and who is going to help teach. I told them that when I come back from America in the fall, I will have someone with me to help start a school. They plan to go down and get the rest of my stuff at the airstrip, or more of it anyway, sometime this week.

That's all the news for now.

March 9, 1997

"God made him to be sin for us; who knew no sin, that we might be made the righteousness of God in him." II Corinthians 5:21

This is Sunday afternoon. I put the power regulator back together last night, since the batteries were charged. I have been working on the computer full blast since then. It doesn't seem to be recharging, but I have been draining the power pretty steadily too. They started the Sunday school for the three different classes today. Next week it is my turn to teach the women in the morning and the kids in the main service. It will be my first experience at teaching in Pidgin. I am looking forward to it though. Priscilla, Natoline and I are taking turns. Priscilla did it today. The kids will be harder than the women, because they are so unruly and hard to keep interested; but all the same, I had rather teach kids.

Yesterday I hurt my back. It hasn't rained at all in six days and I went down to the spring to carry two full buckets of water back to the house. It feels like I smashed all the disks in my lower back. I didn't sleep very well last night, even after taking a dose of pain medicine. I had nightmares, all concerning violence done to my back. I can't even put on socks. I hope it gets well soon and isn't permanently injured in any way.

Luke has been gone picking coffee but came back Friday. He left again this afternoon and will be gone until Friday again. I may only have literacy classes Friday of every week, because Saturdays everybody goes to the village Kongorau to play soccer, or watch it played. And Sunday is lotu day. I suppose I could have a class Sunday afternoon.

Luke has been studying the primer I made him, and today he came by the house to showoff by reading out the names of the letters on the verses I had embroidered as wall hangings. I was properly impressed. I told Wimyung that if he wanted to, he could come with Luke to learn how to read, and Jakob too. They were excited and promised to come. They are both about ten or eleven years old I think. Little Paul wants to come too. He's Jakob's little brother, around seven years old. So that will be four.

Not much has happened this week, I studied Pidgin every day, started some trays of peppers and tomatoes, turned up an old garden to replant, wrote some letters which have yet to be mailed, memorized the second chapter of Jonah and caught four rats.

That's all for now.

March 10, 1997

"Every good gift and every perfect gift is from above, and cometh down from the Father of lights, with whom is no variableness, neither shadow of turning."
James 1:17

As I write this, there are still tears on my face, though I laugh and rejoice at the same time. My God is so incredibly, overwhelmingly, incomparably good!!! Only my God can answer prayer with such awesome perfection. May He receive the honor and glory forever and ever, Amen. I just talked to Mom and Dad by phone patch over the radio. Dad said that they had put out an appeal for a man to come teach here and start a Bible school. Dewayne Noel, the son of the missionary Steve Noel, read it and felt called. His wife, Deanna, is standing behind him. If I understood correctly, they are at the present being trained by Milton Martin and will be coming to sit under Dad's teaching for Bible doctrine for two or three months. They probably will be coming back with me by the end of this year. The phone patch was disconnected before we got done talking, but I just fell on my knees beside the radio and laughed and cried and praised God for the answered prayer. The Noels have three small children under the age of six. I'm still a bit stunned. I don't know what else to write. The focus of all my prayers, thoughts, and dreams for the last six months has been suddenly answered in five minute's time. Wow! God.

March 16, 1997

"Dispela hetpris i bin kamap man olsem yumi. Em i stap holi, na i no gat wanpela rong i stap long Em, na Em i klin olgeta Em i save stap longwe long ol sinman, na God i bin mekim Em i winim ol samting bilong skai na i antap moa."Hibru 7:26

Due to the power problems, I'm not able to work on the computer as often as I'd like, and that accounts for the days I haven't kept diary and should have. I shall try to catch up now.

I haven't heard anything more about the Noel family, but I feel like I'm getting to know them simply by praying for them. The people here have slowly gotten more excited about the idea over this last week. Lawrence is the cause of most of the enthusiasm. He is simply overjoyed at the thought of being able to go to Bible school and possibly, one day, even teach. Lawrence is unmarried and nearly thirty, I'd say, though these people look older than they are. He studies more than any of the men I've met so far. He is one of the preachers here and at Kongorau. He doesn't like physical labor or the social life that seems to be a confirmed part of the culture

here. He is somber and serious and stays in his house reading when he is
not out witnessing or preaching. He is also the leader of all the outreach
done, preaching at the Singsings and hiking into remote villages to preach.
This morning, during the service, he was more excited than I have ever
seen him as he struggled to make the people see what a tremendous answer
to prayer the Noel's are and how wonderful it is going to be to have a Bible
school. I was encouraged to see them all respond, and at that moment
knew that God had been working in hearts and minds during the week.

Today was my first time to teach Sunday school, and I did it entirely in
Pidgin, and without a translator. It went far better than I ever expected it
would. There were a few times that I got my grammar tangled. I could see
on a few faces efforts to restrain smiles, but they understood me and were
in rapt attention the whole time. I took two pieces of white material, and
on one I wrote in Pidgin a dozen sins. Then I smeared the "robe" in the dirt
until it was filthy. In large, black letters, across the middle, I wrote SIN-
MAN (sinner). The other one I left white and clean without a mark on it. I
had seven points, relying on the Pidgin scripture to do most of my talking
for me. I started with man's sinful condition, reading a list of sins in Mark.
I then went on to explain that the "payment for sin is death." Next came
the holiness of Jesus Christ, then how He took our place. At this point I
used my talk-picture and demonstrated how Jesus took our robe of sin and
died with it on Him. With the dramatization, even the children were wide-
eyed with attention. I showed Jesus' crucifixion, death, and three days in
the heart of the earth. Then I showed them how he left our sins there in
hell. I took off the filthy garment and threw it roughly in the dirt, turned
and walked away. Then I took the clean white garment that Jesus had previ-
ously taken off, so that He might carry our sins, and proceeded to read
scripture about the free gift of eternal life. In Pidgin, it is called the present nothing (a gift without a cost). I offered the clean robe as the "present
nothing" and the Christians had tears in their eyes, the unbelievers looked
like they wanted to run for their lives. It was thrilling to be able to communicate so well. There is something about being able to give the gospel
story in a language that is not your own that makes you want to throw back
your head and laugh with sheer joy. Next week I'm supposed to teach the
kids. That should be even easier since our Pidgin is on the same level.

Pastor Allen wrote five P.N.G. churches, requesting financial aid in the
building project, and one church responded with K500. I think they were
as surprised as I was. They are all doing well and working hard lately.

Well, I had plenty more to say, but my power warning just came on, so I had better close before I lose what I've written.

March 18, 1997

"It is a good thing to give thanks unto the LORD, and to sing praises unto thy name, O most High." Psalm 92:1

This is Tuesday evening. I just hooked my power back up so that I can run the computer. It hasn't rained in nearly three weeks. Phenomenal for rainy season. There has been a cyclone between P.N.G. and Australia, and it has caused some pretty severe weather disturbance all over the island. Port Moresby had a few deaths and casualties, and the Maranatha Baptist Church and school (The Lindsey's and Beachy's) had the roof torn off. There were over 500 homes destroyed on the island of New Britain and damage all along the coast and on the smaller islands. I haven't heard if the cyclone, known as Justin, has dissipated yet or not. In any case, we still haven't gotten any rain, and the banana trees look like paper confetti from the high winds. The ground is dry and cracked. I have to carry water from the stream every day.

The last few days, I've been making a Thai tier on the hill behind the house. The girls pulled all the kawkaw vines off and burnt it black so it looked really hideous for a while. It was too steep to plant anything but kawkaw on it so I took a shovel and dug three tiers (big steps) and laid rock around the edges. Then I planted yellow orchids on the bottom one, lavender on the middle and yellow and purple orchids on the top one. It should be gorgeous when they are all in bloom. Roses and orchids grow better here than anywhere I've ever seen. They bloom continually.

Home is always on my mind. I think about the good food more than anything. I'm doing a four-day fast right now. Visions of steak and black bread, Mexican food, pizza, and chicken prepared a thousand different ways alternately fight their way into my mind. Somebody said that health, wealth, and sleep are three things that have to be interrupted to be truly enjoyed. I think I could safely add good food to that list. There are some folks here that I will truly miss and think of often. Jerry's family will be number-one on that list. Each and every one of them is special to me. Not hardly a day passes but that six-year-old Jesse throws herself in my lap or wraps around my knees exclaiming, "Ay Yom!" (Big sister!) Four-year-old Sisilya, I always think of as Serious Sisal. She hardly ever smiles, takes everything so seriously. The other day I heard her drop her voice as low as possible to imitate her daddy. She boomingly sang, Hayelluya, dine da glory, Revive us again!" Little Lazarus doesn't talk; he just gives me a sly smile and cocks one eyebrow at me. Jerry and Natoline are always working together, singing together, and laughing together. You can't help but like folks that like each other. She looks about eight months pregnant. I'll also miss Luke, Alice, Rosinda, and all the girls. But I will be so glad to see my own family again. I can't wait to hear some good English preaching. It has been so long since I had any spiritual input other than my own Bible study. I have to admit though, I have really enjoyed the memorization this year. Hebrews was a tremendous blessing, and now I'm really having a blast with the book of Jonah. I will finish it this week. It's so fun to quote with a little drama.

I have put off the bad news as long as possible, but I guess I'd better record it. Priscilla disappeared Sunday night. I got the story from Pastor Allen. He said that she had made a false statement about Rosinda (his wording), something about her going around with Pastor Allen, intimating that the two were trying to start something immoral. Rosinda found out about the statement and was shocked and outraged. She and the other girls all left for Fogefoge and stayed gone all last week in protest. Pastor Allen was blissfully unaware.

Well, Priscilla was just here. She tapped on the house and came in to tell me her side. Before she went home she asked me to pray. She was coming from Simbai hospital where she went with two girls from Kongorau that had met her on the road. She just went for a check-up (she's seven months pregnant). So now I have both sides of the story. I guess I'll combine them. What I said before was true, but it was a year ago. Priscilla said that last year before I came, they had a marital fight and she accused him of flirting with Rosinda. There was no one present, but just as she said it, Jerry and Natoline rounded the corner of the house and heard her. Priscilla retracted what she said and requested that it not be repeated. Pastor confirmed that fact. This last December, six months later, Natoline told Rosinda. Rosinda and all the other girls got mad about it. But except for some cold-shouldering, they still didn't mention it until Priscilla started teaching Sunday school last week. Last Sunday, after the girls returned from Fogefoge, they went to Priscilla. Rosinda threw a bilam on the ground that the girls had been making for Priscilla and told her that she could do her own work and make her own bilams from now on. I guess that was an opening statement, because the real fight followed. Most of the village gathered and the whole, smelly tale came out. Priscilla apologized, said she was wrong, and paid Rosinda ten kina compensation. Natoline apologized for being the talebearer and paid ten kina to Rosinda. Then the girls all shook hands and made peace. Pastor Allen then prayed. As folks started to depart, the girls added, "Also, when Pastor Allen brings good food and clothes from town, you never share them with us, you just keep them for yourself." Then Pastor Allen told them that they were right, that she never shared, and furthermore, she had a room full of clothes and treasures that she should give away, but she was too greedy. Priscilla said that she got really angry. That evening, after all the people were gone, she gathered up all the clothes Pastor Allen had bought her and threw them at his feet, demanding that he go give them to his sisters. She said she was leaving him. He told me that he preached her a sermon about Lot's wife and Potiphar's wife and told her that she was like those two women and needed to humble herself and admit it. She said she'd had all of his preaching she could stomach and told him what a lousy person he was. He said she was welcome to go, he certainly wasn't going to stop her, and he would just stay here and serve the Lord alone. So she left for Simbai while it was still dark and didn't tell anyone where she was going. Pastor Allen came over this afternoon to tell me what a terrible wife God had given him and how she was bound to go wrong since it ran in her family. Priscilla is no angel either, but she knows how to make herself look more innocent than Allen. He incriminates himself worse than anyone I ever met. So she came in and asked me to pray that God would take away her anger toward her husband and help her lay down her pride. I think it's her pride that gets under his skin so badly. She's too untouchable and confident. He is tired of being the Jerk. Oh, well. I didn't say anything to either one of them, nor did I ask to hear the story. I just listened and prayed with Priscilla and sent her home. I hope it all turns out O.K. On that cheerful note, I shall go to bed.

March 23, 1997

"When my soul fainted within me I remembered the Lord and my prayer came in unto thee, into thy holy temple." Job 2:5

I finished memorizing the book of Jonah this week. It is so fun to quote. Anybody going by my house after dark probably thinks the white lady has lost her mind. One moment I am shivering and whining in the belly of a fish, the next preaching in a hoarse voice to Nineveh, and the next, pouting and griping at God because of His mercy. It is the most entertaining thing I get to do out here, memorizing scripture. I learned a lot from that basket-case Jonah too. Most of all I saw the difference in God's attitude toward the sinner and Jonah's (or my) attitude toward the sinner. God knew

things about Nineveh that Jonah couldn't even guess. He knew the depth
of their iniquity and still loved them so much that He went to incredible
lengths to get His word to them so they wouldn't perish. Jonah only loved
himself. He was angry when the people of Nineveh repented and escaped
judgment. He wanted every one of them to die. He blamed God for being
merciful. At first I was shocked at his horrible attitude, but then I had to
stop and think, have I ever neglected to pray for someone that is a real
pain-in-the-neck because I didn't want to do anything to delay or diminish
the judgment that I knew they had coming? Have I never been aggravated
to see the blessings of God poured out on the ungodly? And isn't that the
same attitude that Jonah had? How gracious our God is! Just the other
day I saw two kids, one of them spoiling for a fight. The other one knew
better than to provoke her brother outwardly, because then, they'd end
up sharing the punishment. But she wanted to see her brother get what
he deserved and did so by simply watching him with a superior disgusted
sneer. She gave him the EYE until his rage boiled over and he struck out
and merited a spanking. But she hadn't done anything. Her only sin was in
not sincerely desiring what was best for her brother. She didn't LOVE him.
She learned it from her mother. Sometimes her daddy gets up in the morning and he's in a touchy mood. Not angry, but in one of those swayable
moods that can go either way. And her mama is a good submissive wife.
She doesn't provoke her husband. She simple LOOKS at him with a superior disgusted sneer that is barely discernible. Outwardly she is the perfect
wife, but neither does she sincerely desire her husband's good. What she
sincerely desires is that he be judged of God in front of the whole world
and humiliated. She doesn't LOVE him. How often we humans treat each
other this way. It is the sin of the Pharisees. It is the opposite of the mind
of Christ. How hard it is to sincerely desire the good of someone who is
unworthy. To love the unlovable and forgive the unforgivable. Once again
I stand in awe and amazement at the foot of the cross—that the Creator of
the Universe should love me that much!

    I taught the kids Sunday school today. I taught them about Jonah. Some
of them don't speak Pidgin yet, so I used a lot of pictures and actions.
When I imitated the whale throwing up Jonah, they all scattered on the
floor as if they expected Jonah to jump out of my throat and land in their
midst. For each of them, on a sheet of paper, I had drawn the outline of a
big fish with a man in his belly. At the end of the story I gave them each a
color and told them to color their fish. None of them but Jesi and Sesilia

had ever colored before (they learned how at my house), so I had to show them how to do it. It was the experience of the year for most of them.

I'm hoping someone will go to Simbai tomorrow and get the key to Sasu's store. He's in the Hausik (Hospital) there. I need my food-stuff and crates. Otherwise, it will all be locked up until after I leave. And I'm out of a lot of supplies.

I wrote a song this week called Now I See the Son. It is the story of the blind man in John chapter nine, which I am memorizing now. It takes two people to sing it properly, so I'll have to get Nathan to learn it. I am stuck on the key of E now. It just has the sweetest sound. It's funny that in nine months I have learned to play the guitar better than I ever learned to play the piano, which I practiced for twelve years. It is my only company up here. I spend at least two hours on it every day. I wish I had some books to teach me different picking and strumming patterns and alternate chords. All I've got is one beginner's book that has the basic chords, and I left that behind months ago. My left hand has grown thick and strong from chording.

Well, I ran out of interesting things to say several lines ago, but there is simply nothing to do, except play the guitar, so I am trying to prolong shutting the computer off. I think I'll go for a walk now.

I went for my walk. Jerry was out in front of the house flattening the ground with a shovel. His kids were all around him happily chattering one-sided conversations all at the same time. "Jerry," I said above their happy din, "You are a working man." He smiled somberly and replied, "Knowing how to work is a present that God has given me." Now it would be unusual in the States, but it is unheard of in P.N.G. for a man to consider work to be a present from God. But Jerry works like it is the greatest privilege bestowed upon him. He is slight of stature, but six to eight hours out of every day he is swinging an ax, or carrying a big log on his shoulder, or throwing dirt with a shovel. As a result, he is one quivering mass of muscle. I'd hate to have to fight him. He makes Arnold Schwarzenegger look like Big Bird plucked and greased.

Jesi, Jerry's oldest daughter, went with me on my walk. We went all the way to the end of the gardens. It is the most exciting part of the trail, because you have to balance on slippery logs the whole way. Then we did a little exploring. We started to cross a ditch on a fallen tree that from outward appearances was wide and firm. However, the inside must have rotted to extinction because suddenly, right in front of me, Jesi disappeared from the waist down. It shocked her as much as it did me, but all she did was say in mild alarm, "Oh, it ate me." And truly, the log did not bust or make a sound; it simply opened invisible rubber lips and swallowed her lower torso. Creepiest thing I ever saw. She had to pry herself out, because if I'd gone near we might have both been eaten alive.

Well, that's all for today.

March 28, 1997
"As long as I am in the world, I am the light of the world." John 9:4

Happy Birthday to me! Well, someone ought to say it, don't you think? It is almost over now. My twenty-third birthday. Every year I think, "Wow, God, what's taking you so long?" Surely, He'll return before I'm twenty-four. It wasn't too bad a birthday, considering I'm in the middle of a jungle on the other side of the world from my family. The sun shined, I'm not sick, and I got the wash done. I told Rosinda earlier in the week that my birthday would be on Friday, so she and Lucy had picked bouquets of flowers and made cards to leave outside my door for me to find this morning. I expect Mom and Dad might have tried to phone-patch me, but CRMF is closed for an early weekend since it's Easter Sunday. So I had oats for breakfast and tuna fish salad for lunch and hot tea for supper, and I imagined a big gooey chocolate cake with vanilla ice-cream. I could almost taste it too. Monday I will walk down to the airstrip and pick up my mail, if it is there. That will be my birthday present. A wonderful one too. I haven't had any mail in five weeks.

Last time I forgot to record a very important fact about P.N.G.. There has been some trouble in Port Moresby. They actually booted the Prime Minister on Wednesday. As of now, we don't have a government or a Prime Minister. They are discussing a temporary, caretaker government and an early election. Prime Minister Julius Chan (Chinese) was doing something illegal, hired some mercenaries from South America to do dirty work for the government by eliminating some trouble makers. So they ousted him. The P.N.G. army nearly split over it. The country is divided and fighting, just words so far. Most of the stores in this country are owned and run by Orientals, and so there has been mass looting and rioting in towns. Missionaries and whites are being escorted by machinegun armed guards. Up here in the bush, no one has even heard about it. There doesn't seem to be any danger politically for the future of missionaries, but a lot depends on who the next Prime Minister will be and if he will be pro-Catholic/Anglican or pro-freedom of religion. So that is a very big prayer request in every church in P.N.G. at this moment. The main tension should die down this week, it remains to be seen what they will do about the future running of this country. Pastor Allen hopes they turn it back over to Australia to govern. I don't know if there is even a chance of that. Time will tell.

I think Septimas went to Madang for hospitalization, so my stuff is locked up indefinitely. I sure could use some of those supplies, but I guess I won't starve to death either.

Well, in keeping with past tradition, I wrote a poem on this, my birthday. Actually, I wrote three, two songs and one poem. I'll record here the poem and one song:

Tomorrow's Yesterday

Have you ever, ever noticed how the worries of today
Are about some grim tomorrow that may never e'en take place?
Then rest! Strength is only promised for tomorrow's yesterday.

Have you ever paused to notice how the things you ought to say
You postpone until tomorrow, or some other, better day?
Heed my warning: Say "I love you" on tomorrow's yesterday.

Have you realized - oh, ever - that some distant future day
Is the time that you are planning to the will of God obey?
Oh, be faithful, Friend! Be faithful with tomorrow's yesterday.

When you think of His returning - Yes, that great and glorious Day
Is your hope dim with the waiting of a joy so far away?
Then rejoice! He may be coming on tomorrow's yesterday!

Justice Met Grace

Grace and Justice were their names
Different as the night and day
Never once could those two meet -
It couldn't be.
Justice met the law's demands
Grace reached out a loving hand
Through the years they seemed to be -
Two enemies.
Would Grace and Justice ever meet?
Could they ever both agree?
Would there ever be a time -
Both were satisfied?

One day 'neath a rugged cross
Justice seemed quite at a loss
"The wage of sin is death," he said -
"Behold the death!"
Grace was there, she bowed her head,
Saw the empty tomb and said,
"The gift of God is eternal life -
"Behold the life!"
So Grace and Justice met that day
Satisfied, they went their ways.
Oh, thou blessed, hallowed place -
Justice met Grace.

This last one is a song and it seems special to me. I think if I ever have twins, a boy and a girl, I'll name them Justice and Grace. And that about sums up this tomorrow's yesterday and yesterday's tomorrow. It was as ordinary as they come.

And here, dear reader, the computer ate my diary. Ten minutes later it ate the back-up copy as well. I can't explain its voracious appetite or bring back that which was digested, so I shall attempt to tell the rest of the story as I remember it. Most of the details are lost to my mind, since I have far less memory than my computer, but the main structure of the story is as follows:

The month of April was spent much in prayer and anticipation for the coming of the Noels, and also in dreaming of home. I couldn't believe that after less than a year on the field I would have an opportunity to return home for a visit.

It wasn't until months later that I realized the tremendous emotional strain I'd been under from constantly fighting rejection. Going home seemed like parole from a life sentence. I could see in my people's eyes that many of them thought that I would not come back. Even though they talked about the Noels coming, there were still comments that seemed to encourage me to just go home and not return. Pastor Allen especially seemed determined to persuade me to leave for good. He asked for money continually, even when I felt sure he knew that I would not give it. And at times it appeared that he was provoking me intentionally, hoping that I would blow up and throw in the towel. But God had answered my prayers for more laborers and I was now convinced that prayer worked.

The first day of the month of April, I sat down and wrote a covenant to God—something I had never done before—promising to meet with Him in prayer twice every day during the whole month of April to intercede on behalf of the Kumboi people. I decided to pray for every one in my village by name, as well as all the leaders of the various fellowships. Then I marked out the geographical territory I wanted to claim—Jimi Valley to Aiome. I thought of all the things that Satan could possibly do to deter me in this purpose, and wrote out a statement of defiance and rebuke in Jesus' name. I also compiled a three-page list of every thing and everyone under the sun that I wanted to pray for. It sounds kind of funny now, but I was ready to do war (spiritual war).

Every evening when I was done with memorization, I got out my atlas, prayer list, and covenant and spent an hour in fervent intercession. My house is set a little way off from everyone, and I prayed in a low voice to make sure no one heard. But the pitpit walls are thin, and anyone standing still right outside my house could have heard everything I said. One day Priscilla came over to visit. "Last night some preacher boys came to visit us," she said, "I came over to buy some rice from you to cook for them, but when I came to the door I heard you praying, so I stopped. I thought you would be finished soon, but you prayed for a long time. I heard you pray for all of us by name, and I went back to my house. I told Pastor and the boys what I heard. Lawrence said one night he heard you pray for him, and Steven said he has heard you praying for everyone too. They want me to tell you that by this they know that you really love us and to tell you that God is answering your prayers."

When you really pray for someone, they become a part of your soul, and it is immeasurably easier to get along with them.

For the first time, it wasn't a task to be nice to Allen. It really puzzled him, and he started pausing for a few seconds of conversation now and then when he passed me outside or saw me cooking in my little smoke-house. One day he told me a little more of his testimony and mentioned the name of the Bible school he had gone to in town. The Holy Spirit kept bringing it to my memory again and again until sked [jungle terminology for scheduled] time on the radio. On impulse, I asked my missionary radio friends what they knew about XXX Mission. There was a moment of silence before the reply, "Nothing we can say over the radio." Of course, that immediately alerted me, and the next time I saw Allen I asked him if he had any literature from the school he went to. He gave me a little booklet containing their mission statement. Reading it explained everything.

They had a rule that any national graduating from their school was issued a license to preach, and that license could be revoked if he (the national) cooperated with anyone outside the XXX Mission structure. They believed that only the white missionary had the authority to start Churches, baptize, and ordain other ministers, and that a native should not be given authority. If the national pastor did not comply with this rule, his "license to preach" would be taken away.

The next radio sked time, there was no one up but the one missionary, and I told him what I had just discovered. He said that XXX Mission was a thorn in the side of many missionaries because of their refusal to let the nationals minister outside of their Mission's jurisdiction.

I prayed and meditated on it for a day. When Allen came by again, he asked me if I agreed with everything in the XXX Mission statement. That was an obvious open door, so I told him no, I did not. For about two hours we talked and I explained that most Christians believe that the Holy Spirit can do the same thing in and with a national pastor as He can in a white American pastor. I told him that The Church at Cane Creek sees Allen Gami Akij as God's chosen leadership for the Kumboi people—not some white missionary who is a foreigner.

Allen looked like I'd dumped ice water on him. That day and for the next two days he kept coming back to tell me bits and pieces of his story.

When Allen graduated from XXX Mission school, they brought him into the office, handed him a license, and told him that if he ever left their authority, his license would be revoked. From that time forward, he never received a letter of encouragement or a friendly visit from the folks at XXX Mission.

On one occasion, the white missionary who was running the Mission at that time came up to their mountain to preach a revival. According to Allen, the missionary griped and complained at the way they were running things, and raked Allen over the coals for daring to start fellowships in various villages among the believers. Then he went back giving negative reports about Allen's work to his friends in town. Allen had stored up a lot of hidden hurt and resentment.

Later, when the XXX Mission heard I was coming, they sent word to Allen that if he allowed me to come, they would revoke his license to preach. Allen got scared. As far as he knew, 90% of all Christianity was the XXX Mission, and I, a lone female, was some kind of off-brand cult. He reasoned though, that if I were like most whites, I wouldn't be able to tough it out for very long and would soon leave on my own. In the meantime, maybe there'd be some financial gain. So he waited, and waited, and waited. And I stayed, and stayed, and acted as though I intended to keep staying.

More threats came from XXX Mission. Allen was afraid he would lose his license and therefore the right to minister the gospel. He decided to be a thorn in my flesh and see if he could irritate me beyond my point of endurance. As he told of his campaign to run me off, I was relieved to discover that it wasn't just my short tolerance level that had caused the stress. And the letter he had written Dad, saying that I either had to leave or pay a large sum of money, was all part of a plan to get rid of me so he wouldn't lose his license. I learned that it was at about the same time that he was getting frantic that I had asked for any literature on the XXX Mission.

It took him several days to tell his story, a little bit at a time, but the change in Allen was enormous. He told me that he had been studying the Word and looking for anything on license. Of course, there is nothing in the Word of God about a man being licensed to preach. Like the church of the dark ages, he had been led to believe that the ecclesiastical powers were the authority of God. With this new revelation, he was going through his own reformation.

After a few days of study and prayer, he came to understand his authority as a believer in Christ Jesus. His burden and bondage fell away. With a bit of a swagger, he told me he intends to take his license to town and hand it to the missionaries and tell them that he doesn't need it or want it any more. "These are my people," he said, "nobody can take them from me or me from them. I am their leader and always will be until my son is grown. I am also a preacher of the word of God by the will of God and not man."

I asked him to write a letter of welcome to the Noels and have the preachers in every fellowship sign it as a seal of their acceptance of Dewayne and Deanna Noel. He enthusiastically agreed that this was a good idea. He prepared the letter and, the last few days before I left, made the rounds to all the fellowships. The first three villages enthusiastically agreed and put down their Xs, but four would not cooperate. They sullenly stated that they wanted me to leave and not come back. Allen talked and pleaded and explained to his wit's end, but they remained unmoved. Why? One of the first boys that got saved under Allen's ministry, some nine years before, was the only other one to go to the XXX Mission school in town. His name is Rufus, and he graduated from school at the beginning of this year. They gave him a license to preach and warned him not to depart from their structure. They told him that Allen had fallen into some kind of cult and that they were going to revoke his license. They warned Rufus not to participate. So when Rufus returned to the mountains, he secretly led four villages into joining him and leaving Allen's authority. He convinced them that Allen was wrong and warned them away from following him. It was all a surprise to Allen—a heart-breaking surprise, I'm sure. He had poured his life out for those people, and Rufus himself lived with Allen for years while Allen discipled him.

Allen sat at my table and wept with discouragement at the blow. I was almost ready to offer to leave for good when he raised his head and said, "Any time God starts moving, Satan starts moving too. I know that I have done the right thing and I will not turn back even if I'm the only one left standing on my side." I was so proud of him then, and I know God was too. Later, after thinking about it, he said that when Dewayne came and started teaching, the others, who were now resisting, would eventually come to get the good teaching.

April was gone, and I spent the first few days of May packing and cleaning the house. I sold all my extra food and locked up my belongings in the storage room. I gave the key to my house to Priscilla and asked her to look after my stuff. The Aikram family hung around with mixed feelings the last few days. They were excited for me to be able to go home and see my family again. I was astonished at the insight and understanding there. The mothers especially kept imagining out loud what Mom would say when she saw me again and how happy I would be to see my brothers and sisters. Then they would mourn for themselves and mourn that I was leaving them behind. The favorite joke was to saunter up with a bag swung over their shoulder, throw an arm around my waist and announce to the crowd that they were going to America with Rebekah. Several of them did that and the appreciation for the joke just got greater each time. I must admit, it was pretty funny imagining Papa Bill in Wal-Mart for the first time or going through L.A. customs.

All of the girls went with me to Fogefoge on Sunday afternoon. It was raining sideways and no amount of banana leaves or umbrellas could keep us dry. Mud and water were pouring off the mountainsides and onto the trails as we marched determinedly through the storm. It was by far the easiest trip I ever made – I was going home. We reached an abandoned hut at Fogefoge to stay the night and all nine of us camped out there. It was infested with huge spiders that dropped from the "ceiling" with a thump. Twice I served as a landing pad. The next morning we hiked down to the airstrip to wait for the plane. It came, but the weather was too bad for it to land. I trudged back up the mountain to our abandoned hut. Another night with the spiders. Back down again the next morning. It was a lovely morning, all bright and clear, but the plane was busy until afternoon and by then the sky was full of clouds. I heard the plane circling once…twice…three times. And then he was gone. I sighed at the thought of another three hours up the mountain as I shouldered my pack and turned weary feet toward the trail. Then came the sound of a chopper through the angry black clouds. It looked like a giant mosquito landing there among the natives. Two Australian businessmen got out and started speaking to the crowd about gold mines and telling them that they were interested in buying land to start a gold mine in the area. I noticed the pilot still in the helicopter and went down to talk to him. It was a government-hired helicopter from Hagen. He said that if the business men didn't mind, he could squeeze me in and take me to Hagen, but I'd have to find my own way from there. I must have looked pitiful, because the businessmen didn't mind. Before I knew it, the ground was receding as we rocked our way gently up through the clouds. They wouldn't let me pay for the chopper ride and once in Hagen I found a genial-looking old native to help me carry my luggage to the Air Nugini hangar. We exchanged stories in Pidgin and he gave me the nicest compliment I'd had in ages. "Missus, you must have grown up in P.N.G., you talk Pidgin like a native." At the Air Nugini hangar I managed to beg my way on the next flight to Moresby that afternoon. By evening I was with Raymond and Susanna at Maranatha Baptist Church in Port Moresby. I was thrilled to see them again. They had been there six months helping the Lindseys. I was able to spend a week with them there and it seemed like halfway home. Finally, the second week of May, 1997, I returned to Pleasantville, Tennessee. It was great to be home. You can't really be patriotic unless you've lived in another country for a while. The American flag never evoked the same proud, fierce joy that it does in me now. And the word 'home' has become a vocabulary in itself. God forbid that I should ever take my country, family, or home for granted again.

I traveled and told my story to churches, mission conferences, and homeschool groups all over the States during June, July, and August. I met the Noels and was awed again at God's grace and wisdom. They are the people for the job. We talked about the future for the Kumboi people and set about getting the Noel's visas. They have decided to go by faith. Which means no deputation. We will leave when the visas arrive – hopefully before October. Also this summer I've been working on getting this diary printed and making a cassette tape of the songs God gave me in the village. My plans for the future are to return with the Noel family and continue literacy work. I may also be doing some translation work, such as tracts, teaching materials, and correspondence courses.

And at present I am seated in our office building typing this prologue to my diary so we can get the whole thing published. It is so odd to read back over my story and realize that it's really mine – if you know what I mean. Whoever would have thought ordinary Rebekah Pearl would some day have a story to tell? I can almost hear God whisper, "That's what happens when you work for me."   ❖

Rebekah's Update 2008

Many of you have wondered what has happened to me since the writing of this diary… From Papua New Guinea, I went to Israel and worked in a Christian hostel for a year where I ministered to travelers, mainly young people, from around the world. Due to extreme illness, I finally came home to rest and recuperate, and while home, married Gabriel Anast in the summer of 2000. During the following eight years I gave birth to five wonderful children: Joseph Courage, Ryshoni Joy, Hannah Sunshine, Elijah Music, and Chaiyah Eve. Gabe and I currently live in the Southwest and are very busy running our online forums www.welltellme.com and www.7xsunday.net. A CD or tape of the music I wrote while in PNG, titled *From the Ends of the Earth*, is available at No Greater Joy Ministries. There is no other Rebekah's Diary planned, but I am writing new music which I hope to record someday soon.

After I left PNG, Dewayne Noel and his family moved up on the mountain where I had lived. The Bible translation work (done by several others and compiled) was sufficiently finished for the purpose of being able to give the Gospel and teach needed Scripture. Dewayne took on the task of teaching Bible and discipling a group Kumboi men in the Gospel so that they could lead their own people. He was there two years, then felt his work was done, and returned to the U.S. The native men went their separate ways to reach their own people, start churches in their areas, and carry on the teaching of other men, so these men could, in turn, teach others. The Bible school had served its purpose and was closed. When Dewayne made a trip back to check on the church there, he found that eight churches had been established and all but one were doing very well. The one church had come under the influence of a woman who was a witch in that community, and was rendered impotent for the Gospel. Pastor Allen is ministering in a coastal city and doing all right, as far as we know.

The last we heard, which has been a while, the seven churches in the PNG mountains are strong and are active in evangelizing, discipling, teaching and preaching. I would ask the reader to continue to remember the Kumboi people in prayer, as I do.

"I have no greater joy than to hear that my children walk in truth"
III John 4

DEAR READER,

This story of what God is doing among the Kumboi people is still continuing. Your prayers can be a vital part of this ongoing movement of God. It is our desire here at No Greater Joy Ministries that the reading of this diary has provoked many to respond to God's call to take the gospel to every creature. God is standing by with sufficient grace and provision if we will only step out by faith.

We recognize that it is very unusual for one girl to go out alone. It is not our policy to solicit or encourage other females to do so. Rebekah was obeying an unmistakable call from God. God sometimes does the unusual for his own glory. Where were the men when the Kumboi people needed a witness?

If you would like to receive a free monthly publication which sometimes features articles on Rebekah, as well as other missionries, send your name and mailing address to the address below. Rebekah has a CD of songs she wrote while on the mountain in P.N.G. Other books and CDs are available as well. We will send a complete listing upon your request.

Address all correspondence to:
No Greater Joy Ministries
1000 Pearl Road
Pleasantville, TN 37033